ENDORSEMENTS

Cowgirl Up! is the culmination of Wendy Bohling's career journey to give voice to the challenges faced by women navigating a male-dominated business environment. With a huge heaping dose of strength, sass, personal stories, and sharp wit, Wendy demonstrates that our struggles with inequality need not define who we are and how we respond.

Jean Becker, Managing Director, Accenture

This is not just another book preaching about gender inequality. I always groan when the topic of diversity comes up, because many women use their gender as an excuse for not being as successful as they'd like or an opportunity to preach self-entitlement. *Cowgirl Up!* is a refreshing change. Wendy tells real stories that illustrate the challenges and benefits of creating gender diversity. This book was written with the intent of helping women navigate the corporate world. But the real value for executives is to better understand that a diverse team is a superior team. Who doesn't want to be on the best team?

Sandi Mays, EVP, Zayo Group

Cowgirl Up! combines your best mentor advice and executive career success insights into one powerful package. Wendy inspires, motivates and empowers you to cowgirl up to your best self.

Morag Barrett, author of *Cultivate. The Power of Winning Relationships* and CEO of SkyeTeam.com

Wendy Bohling shows her readers how to kick some ass, take some names, and cowgirl up! Bohling offers a slew of practical tips on how women can harness their full power to create fulfilling professional lives, despite the very real challenges they face. Her passionate, self-assured voice not only helps readers to envision positive outcomes for their professional lives—it also provides a solid framework for Bohling's vision of "1+1=3," where men and women work together in the spirit of cooperation and collaboration.

Debra Fine bestselling author: *The Fine Art of Small Talk How to Start a Conversation, Keep It Going, Build Networking Skills - and Leave a Positive Impression* (Hachette)

Wendy has created an engaging book with keen insights and advice gleaned from many years in a hi-tech world dominated by Y-chromosomes. It is a book I would certainly recommend to my 3 daughters, but also one that my fellow Y-chromosomes should read!

Michael Frendo, SVP Engineering, Polycom

Cowgirl Up! is an insightful read about the challenges facing women in business today. I identified strongly with the honesty of Wendy's personal work experiences, both good and bad. I truly appreciated her no-nonsense advice for navigating the male-dominated corporate world. Her down-home, cowgirl approach will have you laughing while thinking deeply about the big issues many of us confront.

Jane Miller, founder of JaneKnows.com and author of *Sleep Your Way to the Top (and other myths about business success)*.

Cowgirl Up! may be written for women in business, but men will benefit from reading it as well. The book will prompt readers to honestly access gender biases of their own and reflect on times they've been the target of such biases. The author's candid sharing of her story adds a personal touch to her advice for navigating the corporate frontier with integrity and professionalism.

Don't just sit there. Cowgirl Up! and read this book!

Pat Patton, Senior Vice President, Nursing Operations, Catholic Health Initiatives

---

Wendy's story is a lively account of moving through adversity with purpose. In the process, she found her authentic self and her passion to encourage others. Her sense of humor is evident as she highlights important aspects of leadership empowerment.

Rosalie Chamberlain, author of *Conscious Leadership in the Workplace*

As the father of a young woman, I believe *Cowgirl Up!* is an important reference for any woman in today's corporate environment. Wendy provides the refreshing perspective of a professional woman navigating the male-dominated business world. Her recommendations regarding business networking, leadership development, emotional intelligence, and courage are invaluable for any professional, regardless of their gender. These lessons are delivered through real world stories from Wendy and other female professionals, which makes *Cowgirl Up!* an engaging and entertaining read. Wendy's passionate and cheerful approach to helping female professionals achieve success is infectious and highly motivational. Cowgirl Up, Wendy!

Tod Baker, Co-Founder and CEO, MDValuate

Cowgirl Up!

A Woman's Guide

to Navigating the Corporate Frontier

Wendy Hall Bohling

To Crystal,

Saddle up cowgirl!

Wendy Hall Bohling

Published by Redboots Publishing, LLC
PO Box 270022
Louisville, CO 80027

Printed in the United States of America.

ISBN-10: 0-9977598-0-1
ISBN-13: 978-0-9977598-0-8

DEDICATION

To my mom and dad, Paige and Frank Hall, who taught me to be the woman I am today.

To Woody, my twin, who pushed me to go big or go home, and to Tina, the sister who taught me to color outside the lines.

To my daughter, Madi, who came out of the womb with all the sass and spunk that I came to embrace much later in life.

To my son, Zach, who as my firstborn was the first bronco I tried to break. Thank you for teaching me that it's your journey. I love you, Zach and Madi.

To Chris Deboer, thank you for loving me for who I am instead of in spite of it. This book would never have come into being without your relentless loving nudges and faith in me. I am so lucky to have found you in the second act of my life.

CONTENTS

ACKNOWLEDGMENTS

Thank you, to my cowgirl posse: Morag Barrett, Sherisse Hawkins, Michelle Weidenbenner, Liz Coker, Carol Ross, Juli Duffer, Renata Corlett, Shawn Carrigan, Jennifer Joyce, and the amazing Coolest Women in Tech group for your relentless support and faith in my crazy-ass journey to become an author.

To my best friends, Robyn Pemberton and Brenda Gaide, who I would never want to do life without, and who are my chosen sisters.

To my favorite cowboys, Garry Kepley, Mike Ross, and John Biggs, who have embraced my crazy and helped me keep the faith in the opposite sex with the way you show up in your life.

To all those who I have had the pleasure and joy to work with and meet throughout my life. You have each touched me and helped me to grow into a better person.

CHAPTER ONE

THE CHALLENGING FRONTIER

Wendy's Words

If not me, who? If not now, when?

A woman with a voice is by definition a strong woman.
But the search to find that voice can be remarkably difficult.
Melinda Gates

This book has been a journey to give voice to professional women as they navigate the male-dominated business environment. However, it would never have been if I hadn't suffered the humiliation of being fired from a Fortune 100 company after suffering retaliation for reporting sexual harassment.

Novelist and freelance journalist, Chuck Palahniuk, says, "Your past is just a story. And once you realize this, it has no power over you." Traumatic events in our lives become defining moments that push us outside our comfort zone to the next place we're meant to go. Coming to terms with the defining moments takes time and an attitude of gratefulness that we think impossible in the moment.

This book is my voice and reflects my personal experiences, but it's important to start by summarizing the gender inequality problem. You can only make best use of your present by understanding your past.

HOW THE HECK DID WE GET HERE?
AND WHY ARE WE STILL THERE?

When our nation began in 1776, women could not own land or vote, and they rarely worked outside the home. Political action brought women the right to vote 144 years later; war put women in the work force.

One of the earliest advocates for women, President John F. Kennedy, signed the Equal Pay Act in 1963, more than fifty years ago. At that time, women earned fifty-nine cents for every dollar earned by men, they weren't allowed to have a credit card in their name, and sexual harassment was not illegal.

While it is easy to scoff at how dismal gender equality was in the past, equally miserable statistics exist today. Eleanor Roosevelt had high hopes as the chair of President Kennedy's Commission on the Status of Women when she hosted the third meeting of the commission at her home in Hyde Park June 15, 1962, shortly before her death. She shared, "Because I anticipate success in achieving full employment and full use of America's magnificent potential, I feel confident that in the years ahead many of the remaining outmoded barriers to women's aspirations will disappear."

Unfortunately, we haven't made the progress Eleanor had hoped. Slightly over 50 percent have no women in executive positions, according to a Peterson Institute for International Economics and EY study of a 2014 sample of 21,980 firms in ninety-one countries. According to Catalyst, in 2015 only 4 percent of the S&P 500 CEO positions were women, and of executive boards, 16.9 percent were women. With only 1 percentage point of improvement in the pay gap over the last year, women currently earn only 78.6 percent of what a man earns. That's not even a 20 percent improvement from 1963. At this current rate, I have to work sixty extra days a year to make the same money as a man doing the same job. Should a cowgirl get half the prize money for winning the rodeo?

INVITE EVERYONE TO THE PARTY

The business world needs more influential women in executive positions and better gender diversity in the boardroom. I've been the lone woman in the room and felt the isolation for most of my thirty years in high tech.

Emma Watson, actress and United Nations Women's Goodwill Ambassador, said it best in a speech at the United Nations Headquarters in New York September 20, 2014, "How can we effect change in the world when only half of it is invited or feels welcome to participate in the conversation?"

Sandra Day O'Connor, first woman appointed to the U.S. Supreme Court, added to the argument when she wrote, "Society as a whole benefits immeasurably from a climate in which all persons, regardless of race or gender, may have the opportunity to learn respect, responsibility, advancement, and remuneration based on ability."

Both these groundbreaking women spoke about inviting everyone to the party as the right thing to do, but what about it being the right thing for business and innovation?

IT'S ALL ABOUT THE MONEY

No self-respecting corporate trail boss would make a big change like inviting more women to the table without developing a business case showing its importance, so what's really in it for business? Better yet, what's in it for a male CEO?

MORE BUCKS: Gender equality would increase the global GDP by 26 percent or $28 trillion by 2025, according to the 2015 McKinsey research. This amount equals the 2015 combined Chinese and US economies. Our global economy can't afford *not* to get this equality thing done.

LOWER COSTS: 56 percent of technical women leave at the midcareer point, when the loss of their talent is most costly to companies. This is more than double the exit rate for men. One midcareer woman leaving costs a company between $150,000 and $200,000, according to the National Council of Women in IT (NCWIT) website. Our businesses can't afford *not* to have 56 percent of their female talent staying.

BETTER RETURNS: Companies with the most women board directors (WBD) outperform those with the least WBD by 16 percent on Return on Sales and by 26 percent on Return on Invested Capital, according to a 2011 Catalyst analysis. Over time, women-friendly board membership benefits increase. Those companies with three or more WBD for four of five years outperformed those without by 84 percent on Return on Sales, by 60 percent on Return on Invested Capital, and by 46 percent on Return on Equity. Companies can't afford *not* to have a more diverse boardroom.

MORE BUYERS: Women make 70 to 80 percent of the buying decisions (thefemalefactor.com). Businesses are missing the person who understands their buyers the most. In terms of innovation, corporations can't afford *not* to include women in their product and service creation teams.

Businesses can't afford *not* to have gender equality. Corporate mavericks must be deeply concerned about what they are missing by not having more women at every level in their business. Role model businesses, where gender equality is the norm, reap benefits to the financial bottom line. They bring innovation to the market, and they attract, grow, and retain great people. Success of these companies will be the magic carrot creating more widespread adoption of gender equality by the laggards.

I'm passionate about gender equality, not only because I'm a woman, but because it's the exact right time to fix this inequity. Margaret A. Neale, Stanford Graduate School of Business professor, noted a decade ago in her landmark scholarly piece on diversity that "The worst kind of group for an organization that wants to be innovative and creative is one in which everyone is alike and gets along too well" (Rigoglioso 2006).

All my life experiences have set me up to work for gender equality. My goal is to increase the number of gender-intelligent businesses and leaders in the world. I dream of business environments where women and men work collaboratively, leveraging each other's strengths and perspectives for phenomenal results.

AND NOW FOR THE REAL STORY

"Stories are just data with a soul," as best-selling author and speaker Brené Brown shares in her popular Ted Talk, "The Power of Vulnerability." We learn differently through stories. They captivate and resonate in our brains in a way that data alone cannot. Stories evoke a sticky emotional response. I've used stories in my sales career to portray a product's impact in a memorable way. I leverage stories throughout the book to share how authentic women leaders are navigating the male-dominated business arena.

CHAPTER TWO

A COWGIRL'S TALE

Wendy's Words

Boldly walk through the doors that open at unexpected times in your life.

If you don't like the way things are going, change it!
If you don't like what your mind is thinking, change your mind!
Anne Richards, late former Texas governor

"Get your butt off that ground! What are you made of anyway?"

I wouldn't let someone talk to me like that, yet I'm usually the one shouting to myself during tough times. I call it tough *self-love*. I've had an incredible life. In all senses of the word, I've been extremely lucky. I had parents who unconditionally loved me and believed in me,

9

a crazy-ass twin brother who motivated me to compete and succeed, a sister who is my constant and best friend, and a history of dream jobs I literally fell into by accident.

However, my luck ran out when I was retaliated against for eighteen months and finally fired after reporting sexual harassment at one of the largest telecommunications companies in the world.

THERE'S ALWAYS A STORY

I landed my first job, which I thought would also be my last job, right out of college. I'd like to tell you this job offer was part of a logical, methodical plan, but the truth is actually far more interesting.

As a broke college student at the University of North Carolina at Wilmington, working in a fast-food seafood restaurant was anything but glamorous. And when I say less than glamorous, I am being extremely charitable. Spend all day up to your elbows in fish grease and see how glamorous you feel (and smell). I would stop smelling of grease about the time I started my next shift, and believe me, "*Eau de Fried Seafood*" is not a strong turn-on for guys. But it paid the rent.

When the restaurant cashier learned I was majoring in math, she asked why I wasn't tutoring. With the incentive of retiring my greasy apron, I made a dozen low-budget marketing flyers with tear-away strips containing my name, phone number, and a nifty description of my services: "Math getting you down? Call Wendy for some help."

My most lucrative idea was when I advertised my services to the local high schools and at the college. Tutoring opened doors to my future, allowing me to catch a glimpse of my passion for motivating people.

IT'S WHO YOU KNOW

I tutored Trish, a nontraditional math student returning to college after working for a couple of years. We hit it off and became good friends. She was a bridesmaid in my wedding and the gatekeeper to my business future. Trish convinced me to send a resume to her dad, a bigwig at a large telecommunications company.

Unfortunately, I had no resume. I had skipped the typical senior resume-creation exercise because I was accepted to the Wake Forest graduate program in hopes of becoming a college math professor. I was amazed when my quickly drafted resume got me a plane ticket to Chicago and an interview.

They offered me the job on the spot. I don't even remember talking during the interview, especially since most of it was technically over my head. I remember nodding and trying to look intelligent.

On the flight home, I cried. The motherly lady in the next seat asked me what was wrong. I told her I was coming back from an interview, and she asked, "You didn't get the job, honey?"

Through my sobs, I clarified the reason for my tears. Being offered the job presented a great opportunity. I wanted to take the job, but it meant moving away from my family, something I hadn't remotely considered in all my strategizing for the future.

In a blink of an eye, I was off to the Midwest, all by my lonesome, to be the next big-shot engineer.

WHAT YOU HIDE COULD BE YOUR BIGGEST STRENGTH

Years as an engineer brought tremendous professional growth and a Texas-sized personal *Aha*. I was an extroverted engineer, not common in a product organization. Have you heard the joke about extroverted engineers? They look at your shoes instead of their own. I only checked out people's shoes to see if they were stylish enough to warrant a shopping trip to acquire a pair. As an extreme extrovert, I looked people straight in the eye.

Over my many years in engineering, I felt like the lone buffalo in the herd of cattle. There was a constant undercurrent of criticism. *Don't stand out too much. Tone it down. Be a little less.*

Once, I scooted my chair closer to an employee as I presented his performance evaluation. My action was intended to convey my desire to support him in his professional success, but he immediately scooted his chair away as any normal introvert would. I was seen as a maverick, saying what needed to be said, though perhaps not in the most politically correct fashion. Political correctness was a skill I would acquire over time.

I remember speaking up at a manager's meeting with our CEO. I wanted to see if he was aware of the unfairness in raise distributions created by the performance management tool. About 70 percent of my department did not receive raises due to inconsistencies in rating calibrations. The corporate intent was to have the bottom 30 percent not get raises, far from the 70 percent I was experiencing. I spoke with passion and courage when raising the issue, but I'm uncertain what it cost me professionally. It may have been the first step to my demise.

YOU CAN'T BE IT IF YOU CAN'T SEE IT

In hindsight, I realize I was quite the misfit. At our company's women's conference in Denver, my first hint came while listening to Anne Richards, former Texas governor. She said, "If you don't like the way things are going, change it!"

It wasn't only her words that left an impression; this woman was memorable. I identified with her. She was like me: spunky, a Southerner, and not afraid to speak her mind. Here was a successful woman who was entirely, utterly herself. She thrived in the political arena, outnumbered by Texas cowboys with ten-gallon hats. She was her own cowgirl. She was feminine and powerful; she dressed like a woman, not a woman pretending to be a man. Not only was she comfortable in her skin, she oozed with the confidence that people were lucky to have her in their lives. She was living her life exactly like she wanted.

Anne Richards was my role model and the instigator of my first big uncomfortable moment. She made me feel the internal struggle to be authentic in whatever world I found myself.

I was inspired to be the maverick horse in the corral. I led the 180-person team that built that first Voice over Internet Protocol (VoIP) system, catapulting us into market-share leadership.

I created a culture of openness in the project, routinely asking for feedback to improve my leadership while providing feedback to the company on how we could be better. I initiated conversations across our leadership group to bring more consistency to how we did performance rating. Employees should never be rated higher because of whom they report to. Yet speaking up led to conflict.

Sometimes I felt like the Indian in Buffalo Bill's Wild West show. I fear that standing up for what I believed in ultimately resulted in my being fired and escorted out of the building with only the explanation, "We are unable to find a position in the company where you can be successful."

This event was not in any part of my dream of making it big.

SIT HERE AND QUIT, OR COWGIRL UP!

I had tangled with the big corporate political horses and been thrown. At two in the afternoon, I sat in my pajamas, eating butter pecan ice cream out of the carton with a spoon, sulking because life wasn't fair. Doing an exceptional job was irrelevant if the person in a position of power wanted you gone.

While flipping through the channels, I happened upon a 1994 rodeo movie, *8 Seconds,* directed by John G. Avildsen and starring Luke Perry in the role as Lane Frost, a real championship bronco rider. During the championship ride, Lane is not only bucked off, but he lies motionless on a makeshift table after being stomped in his private parts. I expected his best friend to show the concern warranted by the dire situation, but instead he utters these words: "Well you have two choices. You can sit here and quit, or you can cowboy up. Get out there and show them what you're made of." This was the first time I heard the phrase *cowboy up.*

It reminded me of my dad's saying, "It's not what happens to you, but how you respond to it." I used to think he was talking about those important letdowns in life, like when a guy didn't like you or you didn't get a job you desperately wanted. His words had new meaning to me because of the hell I was suffering in my job. I couldn't believe after decades and three promotions things could turn sour so quickly. As my dad said, though, "It's not the fact you're fired, but how you deal with it."

HINDSIGHT IS TWENTY-TWENTY

As I reflected on my career as a woman in technology and business, I realized other women struggled with the same challenges and issues in the male-dominated business world.

I've interviewed nearly fifty amazing female and male executives to bring additional insight. Their journeys confirm it remains a tough, lonely world out there at times for women in business, but more importantly the interviews revealed stories of women making exceptional impact and finding their right place and fabulous men who support them. I need to share what I've learned. These difficult life lessons are the inspiration for this book.

It has become increasingly clear that sexual harassment and sexism in the workplace continue to be significant barriers to women's success. Being a professional woman brings tremendous fulfillment, but it includes those moments when you're lying motionless in the dirt after being kicked in your private parts. At those moments, chanting your own Cowgirl Up mantra is mandatory to move to a better place.

What's at stake if you don't Cowgirl Up? Will you have enough money to retire, or will you be forced to work until age seventy-five? Will you have the funds to invest in a twilight career passion or help a well-deserving cowgirl get her business started without giving away hard-earned equity to the male-dominated investment community?

Being the trail boss of your destiny is my hope for you as much as it has been my own personal journey.

CHAPTER THREE

INTEGRITY: THE BARBED WIRE OF BUSINESS

Wendy's Words

Integrity means doing what is right in your heart and what is right for the company.

Never doubt that a small group of thoughtful, committed citizens can change the world, indeed it is the only thing that ever has.
Margaret Mead

You're a boring cowgirl if you've never gotten yourself in a tricky situation. Always striving to acquire new life skills, I volunteered to help friends fence their horse pasture on their 354-acre ranch. It seemed a great way to live out my cowgirl persona while enjoying the magnificent panoramic views of the Sangre de Cristo Mountains outside Westcliffe, Colorado.

I had never handled barbed wire in my forty years on earth. I knew this because it makes a distinct impression that I would most definitely remember. What makes barbed wire special is the barb. Working with barbed wire looked relatively easy at first. There were big gaps in the wire with no barbs. It *should* have been easy to grab the wire in those seemingly large areas between the barbs.

As the novice cowgirl, I worked carefully and cautiously at first. As I became more confident, I worked more aggressively, almost with a cocky demeanor until suddenly I was caught, barbs dangerously close to my most private areas. Building that barbed wire fence was like working in the corporate world.

WHATEVER YOU DO, DON'T LOOK DOWN

Climbing the corporate ladder looks easy when you're starting out. There is ample space on the rungs. It's easy to do the right thing. You're working most of the time with the worker bees of the company and first-level management. However, after you have climbed to a certain point, doing the right thing becomes as tricky as working with barbed wire. The visibility you gain higher in the corporate hierarchy can prove to be friend or foe; if you aren't in the circle of trust, those barbs can strike without warning.

Robin Szeliga was forty when she broke into the executive suite at a Fortune 200 telecom company and came face-to-face with the harsh reality of the corporate world. Looking back, she confesses, "Taking that job was the worst choice I ever made. Ego made me take it. And thinking I could fix what was wrong and make a difference. Growing up on the farm, I knew the value of hard work. But I had a lot of blind spots. God told me about my blind spots in the middle of this highly intense role, when I found out I had a detached retina and might lose the sight in that eye. It was clear what I was supposed to understand: *You can't just work hard and be blind to what is going on around you.*"

Robin learned the hard way the cost of being out of alignment with your values. Her career and her health took the full brunt of it. The most difficult experiences present the most significant opportunities to learn. Her advice from a space of learning from her past is, "State your case in an authentic and real way, standing in the uncomfortable zone that it might put you in, and doing it anyway. That's walking the talk."

IT'S ALL ABOUT THE VALUE WE BRING

My own barbed wire experience with walking the talk centered on integrity. I grew up in Virginia with my dad, "Mr. Integrity." He was the original "Abe Lincoln and the penny" of McKenney, Virginia. There has never been a more genuinely good person in my life. A man of few words, each one he uttered held a powerful truth. *Lie* was a cussword in our home. Dad taught us early on that honesty and integrity were all we have in the world.

How I respond to the corporate world is rooted in being clear about my own values. One of the most important factors in determining personal values is how we were raised.

An impressionable leadership class had me writing down my values, or as the leadership coaches more eloquently phrased it, *what I stand for*. Easy exercise right? Maybe as easy as handling barbed wire seemed at the beginning. It's easy to stream together a list of stuff that you'd like to live by: honesty, truthfulness, authenticity, etc. What's challenging is getting down to the ordered list of the top five values that drive your decisions when in a bind.

THE PATH NOT TAKEN

There is a great card game used to help you identify your values. The card deck has a value written on each card (spending time with family, integrity, fun, responsibility). The task is to scan through the deck and choose sixteen cards representing your top values. The process continues by streaming quickly through the remaining deck to reduce the number of cards to eight, then finally four. What is so enlightening about the exercise is *choosing* between values. I say *choose* because this is where you learn the most about yourself. Is it more critical for you to live by honesty or to have a good relationship with God? Advance in the company or build a strong marriage? Tough choices, right? The most enlightening aspect of the exercise is becoming clear about what you stand for, an imperative in those crisis situations where you have to choose which path to take.

Here's a test. Say you've paid for a handful of groceries on a sprint home from work, knowing you can't possibly go one more day without milk, but it's already 6:14 p.m. and there's nothing more frightening than a hungry teenage boy. The change from the clerk includes an extra ten. What do you do? Decision time! What's your core value?

AN ANGEL IN WAITING

My most unforgettable professional crisis not only tested but also galvanized my set of core values. I was supporting one of the top sales accounts through an innovative idea called the "Research and Development (R&D) Angel" program. I loved the name of the program. When else in your life could you have others call you an angel?

The R&D Angel program exposed midlevel R&D executives to our top revenue-producing customers in an effort to drive additional business. I was the first executive of the pilot program before it was deemed official.

During an R&D leadership workshop "customer view" presentation, I met Carol, the account sales lead for my company's top financial customer. I was lucky enough to sit at the same table with her at dinner. Carol and I hit it off immediately. I'll never forget her comment to me that night.

She said, "You don't strike me as someone from R&D. Are you sure you're not in sales?"

When I mentioned my interest in getting more contact with the customer, she said she'd call me about coming to talk with her account. I was surprised when she followed up with me several days later and scheduled a customer visit within the month. I was great in front of customers, and I wanted more customer contact. Carol adopted me. I enlisted support from my management to spend more time with the account, and we developed a relationship.

After a handful of trips, Carol invited me to stay at her home instead of a hotel since she lived a short distance from the customer's location. We had developed a friendship in addition to our professional relationship, making it feel like I was staying with family. Finding ways to minimize the drudgery of business travel helped me stay engaged with this less than glamorous part of the job.

At one of my meetings with Carol's customer, I presented an overview of next-generation communication applications. Afterwards, I chatted with Carol and her boss over a lunch of grilled salmon salads.

Because I have felt intimidated working with vice presidents and CEOs myself, I learned to soften my positional power when working with those below me organizationally—and sitting down to lunch is one of the best ways to do this.

THAT PESKY BARBED WIRE HURTS

As a leader I used the walk-the-halls approach to stay connected to the organization. Once, I spontaneously walked into the cube of one of my female engineers to check out how things were going with her messaging project. I was totally taken off guard when she rose out of her chair as if she were greeting the head of state at an ambassador's dinner. I didn't want that to happen with Carol and her boss. So I carefully planned how to be casual and friendly yet professional with them as we chatted over lunch.

It is important as a leader to maintain awareness of your positional power just as black belts consciously monitor their strength when working with yellow belts. Since Carol's boss was a level below me, I made no exception in this situation. I answered his seemingly innocent chitchat about my lodging arrangements by responding that I was staying with Carol. The conversation took an ugly turn when he alluded to our "having a girl's pajama party." Then he asked what we wear at our pajama parties and finally insisted that he would very much like to join us for that night's pajama party for a three-way. Then he asked if he could videotape the fun.

After many years in the male-dominated telecommunications field, I was in uncharted territory. I felt the blood trickling down as I was struck by yet another barb.

WHATCHA GOING TO DO WHEN THEY COME FOR YOU?

I had often contemplated how I might react in such a crisis situation. You know those situations where someone requires CPR, or there is a need to rise to the occasion and lead folks out after an emergency landing. I've always rooted for the underdog. I remember so many situations where I felt my responsibility was to speak out for good instead of evil by standing up for others. I've always been able to say the tough stuff when it helped someone getting the wrong end of the stick. Yet I found out in that moment that I sucked at speaking up for myself. I have replayed the situation in my head at least a hundred times. This is how it *should* have gone:

I would confidently look the *butthead* sales director in the eye and say with conviction, "I assume that you are unaware that this conversation is quite inappropriate for business colleagues, and I'm certain you did not intend disrespect. I assure you that your behavior is unwanted, and I will expect you to continue in a professional manner consistent with how you should be interacting with two competent female business associates, especially when one is organizationally your superior."

DON'T SIT THERE WITH YOUR CHIN ON THE FLOOR

Instead, my chin hit the floor in utter surprise at the nasty turn in the conversation. I couldn't believe I just sat there. Carol abruptly steered the conversation to a more nonthreatening topic, and we ate our salads as quickly as possible to conclude lunch. I was appalled. How stupid was this guy? Was he oblivious to how inappropriate his behavior was, or did he assume he had the right to hit on us? Unfortunately, I'll never know.

After lunch on the ride back from the city, Carol apologized to me for having to endure her boss's behavior. I wonder how often a male employee would apologize for his female boss's behavior? Carol confided in me how he had spoken to her consistently in the same manner since he joined the company several months before. I pleaded with her to allow us to inform Human Resources (HR) immediately about his behavior. I feared we were dealing with a habitual sexual harasser. He wasn't oblivious to his behavior. He assumed he had the right to speak this way to female associates and even female executives. Carol couldn't have found herself in a rougher spot if she'd tried.

YOU CAN STAY OR YOU CAN GO

I had never dealt with such obvious workplace sexual harassment. We were at the customer site, Carol reported directly to him, and I was a level above him, he in the sales business unit, and me in the R&D business unit. If I had not been so appalled, his nerve might have impressed me. It's like he'd robbed the donut shop directly across from the police station during the breakfast rush.

Carol then told me that she had confronted her boss for similar behavior a few weeks earlier. His response had been to shut down her e-mail access in retaliation. And since her boss's manager had witnessed yet another incident and did nothing to discourage or stop it, Carol was certain her boss would escalate the retaliation if she reported him. She decided her only option was to look for another job outside the company.

I consider myself an inspirational leader. More directly, I can be a tenacious nag in getting others to do what I want them to do. Yet I couldn't talk Carol into reporting the harassment situation. I didn't want this guy to get away with treating women this way. I felt so utterly powerless. As an executive, shouldn't positional power be available in these instances? I was so torn between maintaining the confidentiality of a friend and reporting her harassment. I followed my heart and reported only what had happened to me at lunch to my boss.

A FRIEND IN NEED

Integrity in this case meant not betraying her trust but doing what I could to ensure the company was aware of the situation. I pleaded with Carol almost daily to not allow her boss to get away with his inappropriate behavior, but she maintained her decision that her only recourse was to leave the company. I wish there was a happy ending to this story. Actually, there is a happy ending (for Carol) and a not-so-happy ending (for me).

Carol's happy ending revealed itself after she left the company. She found a great next job and met and married the love of her life. I was the matron of honor in their wedding, and my daughter was their flower girl. Carol's happily married with amazing children.

The not-so-happy ending is that on Carol's last day with the company, with her permission, I reported her sexual harassment to Human Resources. An internal investigation was held, and Carol's boss was found guilty. He was required to take a training course on sexual harassment.

My performance rating was moved from the top 10 percent performance band to the bottom 10 percent performance band. Then a couple of months later I was reassigned from a director to that of an individual contributor with no direct reports. HR's feedback to me was that I couldn't be trusted to manage people anymore. I was disappointed to see that the harasser remained in the same role and level until he left the company two years after the incident.

I'LL LEAVE WHEN I'M READY

Over the course of the next eighteen months, while being moved from assignment to assignment by HR and doing great work, I was consistently rated in the bottom 10 percent performance band.

In my first assignment, my new VP, who hadn't been told by HR why I had been assigned to his organization, was so impressed with the product management project I'd completed that he commented, "I don't know why you're in the bottom 10 percent, but you've done exceptional work and we're getting you into the top rating where you deserve to be."

I had high hopes that this would finally work itself out. But after my new boss attended the cross-organizational performance review meeting, he informed me, "Wendy, you're never getting out of the bottom 10 percent." I was devastated.

Being fired and escorted out of the building by security was tough, but the preceding eighteen months of retaliation took the biggest toll on my self-esteem and confidence.

Many people asked why I stayed. My misguided mantra had been *I'll leave when I'm ready*. They can't force me out. I also had this hope that good would win out, and if I found the right executives to talk to, they would listen wide-eyed to my story then apologize for my having had to go through it, and then right the wrong that had been done. Throughout those soul-crushing months, I was determined to leave on my own terms and not theirs. I was perpetually reminded by HR of my "lack of integrity and judgment." In my heart I knew what I did was right, not only for Carol but for our company and ultimately all women in business. However, standing up for what I believed took a daily toll.

In these types of situations, do what is right in your heart and what is right for the company. It was important for me to do whatever I could to prevent any other woman suffering harassment. I've been asked many times if I would change what I did. I have never hesitated in saying I would make the same decision about remaining loyal to a friend's confidence while reporting the situation as soon as I could to minimize any corporate liability. In hindsight, I would definitely have taken a much more calculated and offensive approach to the situation, possibly leveraging publicity to gain monetary damages for the retaliation.

YOU WOULD IF YOU LIKED ME

Cheryl Campbell, one of the few female executives in the oil and gas industry, recalled her own situation when her integrity was tested. While meeting with a consulting client, it became clear that the client's real agenda was in getting her to share proprietary secrets about how the software worked in her previous company. He knew what he was asking for was a clear violation of confidentiality. She provided only high-level information. He continued to push by asking if she could provide further detail. She clearly stated she couldn't. He again asked what it would take for her to provide the information. She ended the consultation call early.

If you don't have hard moments in your career, you're not stretched to get to the better place. If it's an easy ride, is it worth it? You learn the most about yourself from the tough times.

IT'S NOT THE HORSE YOU RIDE;
IT'S HOW YOU RIDE THE HORSE

That barbed wire can be nasty stuff! I've heard bloody stories of others being fired after standing up to executive teams being creative with their financials or being asked to lie to a customer about a delivery date.

Your integrity and values will be tested in your business journey. You must be clear about your personal hierarchy of values before these incidents happen. It's too late if you have to stop midcrisis and figure out where you stand on a situation. Be wary of corporate politics. Understand that people can be motivated by personal agendas. Do your homework and research how similar situations have been handled before. Never jeopardize your character for others or the business. Know your horse. Know the corporate culture to decide if you want to stay with that one or pick a different horse to ride.

CHAPTER FOUR

SPITTING TOBACCO AND OTHER DISGUSTING COWBOY HABITS

Wendy's Wisdom

Rise above cowboy criticism with your own unique blend of wit and determination.

It's not the trauma we experience that causes the psychic damage, but it's going through the trauma without the right support.
Chet Chavez

You've met them, those coworker cowboys intent on putting you in your place. They're not merely teasing you. There's an edge to their kidding. It's as if they're saying, *Little Filly, remember where you stand in the pecking order. It doesn't matter how important your job title is,*

you're a woman, and you're not as smart as I am. It's not typically overt. It's usually not sexual, but it's most certainly sexist. It's still wrong.

An amazing female CEO, Tiffany Kelly, was hosting a business dinner at her home when one male guest commented, "You live here? You must have a rich husband." Some might say Tiffany was asked an innocent question that should have been brushed off with a chuckle. Here's an equally *innocent* question... "How's that approach been working for ya?"

My college boyfriend chewed tobacco. A few weeks into our relationship, I called him out on this disgusting habit and told him I wouldn't kiss him until he had brushed his teeth after chewing.

Setting this boundary was a memorable example of asserting myself in response to inappropriate behavior. It worked. I never kissed tobacco again. The ability to stand up for yourself is necessary in building credibility and self-confidence. And necessary to stop disgusting behavior.

DISGUSTING IS DISGUSTING

We all know the traditional definition of sexual harassment at work. *Have sex with me, or you'll be fired. I'll promote you if you sleep with me.*

Sexual harassment isn't dead; it's taking on new forms. With social media and more laid-back cultures taking over in businesses, it's more difficult to distinguish inappropriate behavior. A *Cosmopolitan* magazine survey of 2,235 full-time and part-time female employees across a variety of industries reported that one in three women ages eighteen to thirty-four has been sexually harassed at work. The Equal Employment Opportunity Commission (EEOC) receives seven thousand to nine thousand sexual harassment complaints per year. Approximately 84 percent of those complaints come from women. But more disturbing is that 70 percent of women who are harassed don't report it to a manager or an attorney according to that same *Cosmo* survey.

We're faced with more blurred forms of harassment such as sexually explicit or sexist remarks at work. A coworker comments on how nice you look. Is this harassment? If persistent comments single you out for being a woman and make you feel uncomfortable, it contributes to a hostile work environment, the legal definition of harassment.

As women, we don't want to believe we are being harassed or sexually discriminated against. It reduces us to objects. We also don't want to be that uptight woman at work.

Shouldn't we simply shrug off the coworker's constant stories about his sexual encounters? The problem with sexual harassment is that it is emotionally draining and impacts productivity. Being on high alert throughout the day waiting for the next episode and preparing to handle it is not an environment that allows us to flourish.

THE FINE ART OF BEING OBLIVIOUS

I was disturbingly oblivious to sexual discrimination during the first years of my professional career. In the engineering world, gender discrimination can rear its ugly head in less obvious ways, such as having a male boss agree with a male peer's suggestion even though you provided it earlier in the discussion, or being overlooked for a professional opportunity because you're a woman. You can't easily prove it was intentional. God forbid you call them on it. The usual response is denial, or worse, you're told you're overreacting or seeing things that don't exist.

When I was pregnant, it seemed everyone was pregnant. Wherever you looked, there was another pregnant lady. Or after buying a new Honda Accord LX, you couldn't drive to the market without seeing them all over the road. Once you are aware of discrimination, you notice it. It's not that it wasn't happening before! You're just less oblivious to it.

The first step to managing discrimination is to be aware of it. Not as easily done as said though. One of the best ways to increase awareness is to learn about true stories of sexual harassment and sexism in the workplace. Seek out stories from real people. Ask a couple of trusted colleagues if they have ever experienced harassment or sexism. Maybe you're more comfortable researching online to find posted stories of sexism and discrimination.

Once you've strengthened your awareness muscles, tread lightly. To be successful, you must practice a sensitive balance between not looking for the discrimination and not sticking your head in the sand about it happening.

COWGIRLS CHEW TOBACCO TOO

While in a test group of an international product about fifteen years into my career, I expressed interest in an exciting assignment to go to Japan to support our first customer trial.

A few days later, my manager asked me whether everything was all right at home. Luckily our professional relationship was strong enough that he felt comfortable talking to me. Evidently, a peer had raised an issue with our department head, who would decide if I should be considered for the assignment. My coworker had attended the summer BBQ my husband and I throw every year. Many of the folks had thoroughly enjoyed the keg of microbrew we had at the party, but no one, including my husband, was drunk.

The fact that my husband had been drinking must have moved my peer to tell her manager that she was very concerned that my husband was an alcoholic, and with this kind of tension at home, I might not need the additional stress of an overseas assignment. This was an interesting observation considering she was also a candidate for the assignment. It was clear the manager wanted her direct report to get the assignment and used this information to try to sway things in her favor.

I was livid when my manager asked if my husband had an issue with alcohol. My personal life should have no bearing on my professional life unless it is impacting my performance at work. I asked my boss if my performance had in any way altered. He confirmed that he was only concerned about me and wanted to support me with any challenge I was facing.

I told my manager that I appreciated his concern as my friend, but I would expect this in no way to impact my opportunity to get this assignment. I then went to my department head and made it clear how unethical and inappropriate the behaviors of the colleague and her manager were. He assured me that he would handle the situation.

Building strong professional relationships with colleagues who will confidentially tell you about disgusting cowboy situations is the best you can hope for in having the opportunity to set the behavior right. It's also important to know that cowgirls can go to that dark side and see each other as threats as well.

IF YOU SAY NOTHING, YOU'RE PART OF THE PROBLEM

Disgusting cowboys show up everywhere in your life. While introducing myself in a room of men at an industry talk, the male to the right added a little color commentary to my introduction. I wondered why thirty-two men were able to introduce themselves with no such comment.

He asked, "What are you going to do with that little Southern accent of yours?" I quickly replied with a gentle voice and sweet smile, "I don't know, but I think I'm going to have to kick your ass." The room filled with oohs and ahs, like a room full of teenage boys witnessing a gutsy girl diss one of their own.

Calling the guy on his behavior required the same guts and confidence I needed to build credibility in the workplace arena. A professional woman must remember that her ability to be successful is linked to her success in speaking her mind.

DON'T DO OTHER PEOPLE'S DIRTY WORK

I realized the downside to speaking my mind, unfortunately too late. In almost every job, there is that one peer who sees things from the exact opposite as you. If you say white, he says black. I had no tolerance for that guy. Even though he was the glass half-empty guy, I was never sure if he took those extreme positions to deliberately poke me.

During an especially charged staff meeting, our VP laid out a plan to make some priority changes in our product road map. He asked us for our feedback. True to form, my arch nemesis responded by directly blaming my software team for the negative impact his team would sustain because of the changes.

I recall, chanting under my breath, "You can be right, or you can be successful," but I couldn't wait another minute before calling him on his blaming behavior. My exact words were, "You can be in the boat with us to help us figure out the replan, or you can point fingers." Damn, why couldn't I keep my mouth shut?

Later, when the opportunity presented itself with my VP, I gently brought up the situation and asked him why he didn't call my nemesis on his behavior during the staff meeting. I'll never forget his response. "Why should I, Wendy, when I know you will?"

Not the best example of a great leader, but it taught me to allow leaders to be leaders. I didn't have to be the righter of all injustices in the world. I was right in calling a negative team member on his attitude, but I was definitely not successful.

IT'S NOT WHAT YOU SAY; IT'S HOW YOU SAY IT

How you show up in the workplace can make or break your success as much as any technical or business decision.

As my dad often said, "You can live with regret, or you can live with consequences." With age has come the wisdom to live my life with as little regret as possible. How you say something can be more important than what you say.

I remember driving with my dad, Frank, one Saturday afternoon when he was visiting from Virginia for one of my parents' routine two-week stays. He criticized my driving in the most "Frank" of methods. He asked if we were late to get to lunch. I answered that our time was our own today, but why had he asked? He said, "Because you're driving like we are." I snapped back at him with an I'm-not-a-child-anymore-type response. He was visibly hurt.

We rode in silence for a mile until I realized our relationship was much too important to leave the conversation this way, and I apologized for my snippiness. Living with the regret of not making things right with Dad that day would have been too high a price to pay, especially since he died suddenly of a heart attack two weeks later.

Learn to call people on their bad behavior in the midst of a sticky situation with class and maturity. Provide them the ability to save face and hopefully learn from the way you handle the situation.

YOU'RE NOT THE BOSS OF ME

At age sixteen, my daughter, Madi, was forced to call her five male, golf cart-cleaning coworkers on their behavior of treating her like she worked for them. "They tell me what to do like they are my boss," she lamented while threatening to quit after only a month working there.

I cautioned, "If you quit every time a man bosses you around, you'll quit a lot of jobs in your life."

At the young age of sixteen, she was forced to confront the men on their behavior in a way that preserved the relationship.

Everyone finds themselves in sticky situations, but it does feel like I've had more than my fair share of them. I've met with strong, alpha-male men a lot in my line of work, but I was never taken aback as much as during a coffee with a visible and well-known male leader in the local start-up community.

In response to my sharing my book and the mission to get more women in leadership, he didn't beat around the bush. He proudly admitted, "Pushing more women into leadership is like taking minor league players and making them play in the majors."

I tamped down my first response to throw the vanilla latte in his lap and chanted to myself *seek first to understand* a few times as I did my Lamaze breathing to calm myself down. To my dismay, the conversation didn't improve, but what disappointed me the most was recognizing the impact his influence would never make to improve gender equality due to his current attitude. Positional power and influence doesn't bring gender intelligence.

Kathy Hodgson of Lakewood is one of the only 13 percent of women city managers in the country. That 13 percent statistic has nudged higher only 0.1 percent in the last thirty years. She's smart, quick-witted, and one of the most authentic leaders I've met in this incredible journey. She shared some early advice she received from a trusted male leader early in her position. "Every time you walk into a room of men, you have to make sure they know two things: I'm smarter than you think. I'm not interested in sleeping with you." It can be an ugly trail out there, cowgirls.

PRETTY IS AS PRETTY DOES

I wonder if we ever stop being surprised with cowboys' shockingly inappropriate behavior. Growing up with a twin brother, I'm not as easily shocked as the average cowgirl by the more blatant sexist attitude and behavior of men. What really burns my toast is the current-day crotch-grabbing behavior where women are immediately judged based on gender. The appearance of a pretty cowgirl in the corral leads men to the assumption, "She's dumb as a stick."

A CEO of a manufacturer admitted to testing a female salesperson pitching him IT services because he couldn't believe she could be smart. You will be judged on your appearance whether you're pretty or overweight. How you respond can break down the stereotypes one person at a time.

I know that being a pretty girl is one of the nickels I have in my pocket. I spend it wisely. This asset could get me into a meeting, but it's what I do at this meeting with my smarts and talent that mean the most. This is hard for me to admit, but I'm finally in the acceptance stage of the twelve-step program to deal with the hard truth that there are men out there who believe women can't be as smart as men are.

After years on the engineering side of the business, I attended my first conference as a salesperson. My job was to troll the exhibit booths looking for businesses that were overwhelmed in their development pipeline. After a quick conversation with one Bangkok company executive, he offered me a job as their US sales manager. I asked him how he knew I would be any good after talking with him for only ten minutes.

He replied, "All you have to be, if you're a woman in sales, is pretty."

In an effort to take the absurdity to the next level, I asked, "Do you think an attractive *intelligent* sales executive might bring in more revenue than an attractive *dumb* sales executive?"

He looked at me with his head cocked sideways, much like the dog looks at you while you reprimand him for peeing on your den carpet. The smart cowgirl gets better at responding to the nasty cowboy intent on keeping her on the rodeo sidelines.

LIFE IS 5 PERCENT INSPIRATION
AND 95 PERCENT PREPARATION

When I need to be amazing, I resort to the tactic of being excruciatingly prepared. There is no substitute for meticulously doing your homework. This need for preparation was never more apparent than when I was to participate in a competitive landscape panel discussion at a conference several years back. I enlisted my vice president and peers to provide questions in a mock debate to ensure I was ready for the event.

I was pleased with the results and felt ready. Then my VP ended with the comment, "I know you can entertain them, but my boss and I are concerned you don't have the substance to back it up." The confidence hissed out of my body like a punctured tire on a big-ass Ford truck. I wish I had responded with anger, but instead I responded with fear. All I could think was *I'm not ready.*

DON'T GET MAD, GET EVEN (PREPARED)

I once read a research report that asked female, first-year law students why they were having difficulties with their studies. They responded, "We're not smart enough."

In an opposite response, the men in the same classes answered, "The curriculum is too difficult."

I continued to worry I would fail in the panel because I wasn't smart enough until I got pissed. I mean ticked like a cow that's just been branded. Time to Cowgirl Up! Respond to attacks on your ability to succeed with some old-fashioned kick-ass determination. I lay awake for hours that night scheming how I would rise to the occasion and come out swinging on the panel.

THE HELL WITH SENSIBLE SHOES

The next morning while striding through the conference center to the panel discussion, I could hardly contain myself as I made small talk with the fellow walking in step with me. I remarked how we had to walk a country mile to get to the conference facility. He said, "If you wore some sensible shoes, it wouldn't seem so far."

I replied with substance and grit, "You can't kick some butt wearing sensible shoes." I felt like I could climb Mount Everest. I was ready. I was prepared. As I've said, it's not what happens to you, it's how you respond to it. Rise above cowboy criticism with your own unique blend of determination and wit.

AND THE HITS THEY KEEP ON COMING

I have many stories about men's perception of women in the workplace. The more you run up against these nasty cowboys, the less shocked you are by the crappy behavior, and the quicker you put them in their place.

A sassy young professional responded to her boss's comment that she was a filly that needed to be broken by reminding him, "Many have tried."

Unbelievably, I was once asked by a male customer if I "had had any work done up there" while he looked directly at my breasts.

Using my quick wit, I responded with a broad grin, "I've had a lot of dental work done." A general catchall response to all inappropriate comments is, "If you'll forgive me for being rude and not answering your question, I'll forgive you for being rude and asking it."

A spunky young female CEO of an innovative financial funding company traveled to California to pitch to a venture capitalist. He waited patiently until the end of her presentation and shared that he wouldn't be investing in her company. He admitted he had only taken the meeting because she was pretty. Now that's a huge cow pie to be thrown at you.

DON'T MAKE ME TELL YOUR WIFE

I remember the time when a customer said to me, "You're not the typical engineer. You don't have fat ankles."

One female executive recounted a comment made to her, "For a fat girl, you don't sweat much." This really doesn't happen, right? Wrong!

I can top that one. One time at an after-hours professional networking event, I felt someone grab my hindquarters. I spun around and snipped, "That behavior is inappropriate. If you do it again, I'll contact your wife."

At the March 2008 Voice on the Net conference, I visited a vendor's booth. Another attendee, also waiting to talk to the vendor, turned to me and asked, "And where are you from?"

I thought I recognized him and said, "Do we know each other? You look familiar."

He said, "Don't you remember that late night when we were drunk?"

I replied, "I don't recall that."

He said, "I do."

I countered, "I think that was only in your dreams."

Cowgirl Up and use wit to put the nasty cowboys in their place. But be ready for the typical cowboy response when he's been called on his shit of "Don't be so sensitive." A cowgirl's best response in this case is, "Would you like someone talking to your daughter that way?"

In the airport while traveling on a business trip, a male stranger in line behind me at the coffee kiosk asked me, "Who's with your kids?"

I stared back at him with a panicked expression. "Oh my gosh, I don't know. I better check on that."

Businesswomen with no kids are often asked, "Why don't you have kids?" When would anyone ask a businessman that?

YOU MUST BE IN HR

A female director of client services with a high-profile, telecom firm recalls one spitting-tobacco situation. She entered a room of all men for a meeting, and one of them commented to her, "You must be in *human factors*."

Remember those bathing beauties at car shows in front of the flashy race cars? If you can believe it, this marketing exploitation of women is actually still vogue at technical conferences. "Booth Babes" is the common name for beautiful women who are staged in conference exhibit booths to draw more men. Once reined in, the company technical geeks appear and take over the sales pitch.

Is it harassment to leverage salespeople who are attractive? Definitely not. It's harassment only if they are told they must act sexy or, even worse, use sex to get the deal. In 2014, during an interview for VP of Business Development, the CEO told me, "It won't hurt that you're pretty for closing business." The worst part was this CEO didn't even know what he said was offensive.

At least Margaret Heffernan recognized her own spitting-tobacco moment. Margaret, who teaches entrepreneurship at Simmons School of Management in Boston, is also the author of *How She Does It: How Women Entrepreneurs Are Changing the Rules of Business Success.* She recalls, "When I had my first chance to hire my own team, of course I went for the best and the brightest. And they all turned out to be women who were liberal arts majors with birthdays in June—just like me. It's a regrettable aspect of human nature that we tend to like people like ourselves. Maybe the difference is that when I realized what I had done, I thought, oh dear, I must not do that again. Whereas men tend to do it and think, that's fine. They don't see it as a problem."

BEING YOUNG AND A WOMAN—THE DOUBLE WHAMMY

Dee Dee Myers, the youngest White House press secretary in history and first woman to hold the title, was asked if she struggled because she was young. She answered, "Age was part of it. But I don't think my bosses would have given a man a lower rank and salary than all previous press secretaries. Men negotiate starting salaries that are about 7 percent higher than women's. A woman stands to lose more than $500,000 by the time she's sixty." Know your value and demand to be paid for it.

Even the decent cowboys can have double standards when they rate the performance of women differently than men. This double standard is an alternative definition of harassment or discrimination.

During a conversation with my boss, he told me that customers either hated me or loved me. He went on to say, "Men will take crap from men, but they won't from women."

My boss went on to say if I wanted to continue to grow my sales performance, I needed to *figure that out*. An ambitious, hard-hitting female executive is called pushy and aggressive, whereas that same behavior in men is called getting things done and being a driver. What has made me successful is that I challenge my customers and those I work with. I always try to do it with compassion and respect.

GO BIG OR GO HOME

When a customer asked that I be replaced with someone he could work with, I analyzed the situation soliciting as much feedback as I could from those involved. Don't get me wrong. I had my moments of self-doubt—*I'm too aggressive and controlling. I'll never be successful.* That's human. Nevertheless, my success has come from being action oriented and proactively pushing for the close. If you're not pushing hard enough, you'll never achieve exceptional success.

Being safe doesn't work any better in business than it does in NASCAR. Danica Patrick, one of the few women race car drivers, would never have taken first in the 2008 Indy Japan 300 race if she had gone comfortably fast.

Having a customer get his back up occasionally means you're pushing people the right amount. If you've never offended anyone, you're probably leaving money on the table. Take a lesson from Danica: she knows she's pushing her car and her talent because she spins out occasionally.

Of course, if Danica spins out every race, she needs to rethink her strategy. Likewise, if you're offending people routinely by pushing too hard, you need to rethink your strategy.

Achieving success in your business arena means assessing the situation and being honest about how often you're spinning out. Be purposeful and thoughtful. But take risks to achieve the extraordinary. Most importantly, don't let some cowboy's nasty behavior make you second-guess yourself!

THAT WHICH DOESN'T KILL US COWGIRLS MAKES US STRONGER

A cowgirl's success comes from taking the risk and living with the consequences of showing up as a powerful and confident woman in a male-dominated industry and speaking up to challenge a situation when the need arises. Your own success in responding to a challenge is all about how you show up and be uniquely you. Be intentional and purposeful about it.

I hope sharing my personal experiences and those of other hardy cowgirls will help you know you are not alone. Find the strength to confront your greatest fears. Look in the mirror, not to other people, for your self-perception. You will deal with a lot of cow pies in your professional journey. Decide how you want to respond. Shit happens. Deal with it gracefully. Use flair. Be you. God made you a woman, so Cowgirl Up, kick some ass, take some names, and be great.

CHAPTER FIVE

BRAND YOURSELF:
COWGIRL UP TO YOUR PASSION

Wendy's Wisdom

At 50+, I still kick butt. I just do it in killer shoes!

People with passion can change the world

Steve Jobs

Out of frustration and challenge can come clarity about your passion. Or as I call it, your *disruptive strength*. A bronco rider becomes passionate about being the best after being thrown for the hundredth time. When you're lying in the dirt with the wind knocked out of you, Cowgirl Up to your passion.

REBRANDING YOUR KILLER INSTINCT

"She's not difficult to work with. She has a passion for excellence." That's the first time I heard the word passion in my professional life. I was a system tester for a Digital Cross Connect international product and had pissed off a developer by digging in my heels that a problem needed to be solved instead of blown off.

The developer's boss described me as having a "passion for excellence." I was surprised and impressed that he *got* me better than I *got* me.

I was oblivious to my brand. My department head's nickname for me was "Killer." What a reputation! I had acquired a brand of someone who went after the hard stuff and didn't settle for anything less than my own best and the best of others. I was not being intentional about the brand I was building, so I was stuck with collateral damage— being considered outspoken and pushy. A cowgirl's brand exists whether she's consciously building it or not. Be in charge of that brand. Manage it!

About six years into my career, my manager told me I was too aggressive, and she moved me down from the top-rated performance category. She said I made people uncomfortable—and this from a woman. Her comment was my first real memory of biased criticism from a female since I'd never heard a man described as aggressive. I was taught to respect my elders growing up. Elders translated into managers. I assumed she was right and my aggressive personality meant I was bad. I spent two horrible years "being less." I came to work at six a.m. and left at two p.m. with a determination to do the job, don't make waves, and lay low. What a crock!

It took years to come to terms with the *too aggressive* feedback and recognize that the same behavior in men can be seen as assertive. I stand out in a crowd due to my outgoing personality and inability to shut up when things need to be said. This is the definition of assertive. I finally recognized the power of this dimension of my brand being an asset and not a liability.

Understanding that every strength can be a double-edged sword, I spent time dissecting the feedback to see how this part of my strong personality could be a disservice. I realized it might not provide space for others' perspective. Now I am much more intentional with listening and pulling others into discussions. A cowgirl learns to pull the *grain of truth* from the judges' feedback on her rodeo-ride performance and use it to make her brand more powerful and distinctive.

YOU CAN BE GOOD BUT NOT PASSIONATE

I struggled for years in the engineering world wondering what was wrong with me. I was interested in and knowledgeable about technology but not passionate. I loved the early stage of taking on a new project, figuring out the technology, and differentiating our product in the industry. Still, something was missing. The great engineers I worked with were addicted to the technology. The first key to finding your passion is understanding what isn't. Technology was their passion. It wasn't mine.

I love building an organization and culture. I love making a difference in people's lives by helping them find their niche. Joel was a young engineer I promoted to technical manager. He had an uncanny ability to get people to work well together. I approached him about interviewing for my technical manager opening for the new VoIP project, and he got the job. He did a fabulous job building his team as a new manager.

Unfortunately, after about six months, I perceived Joel's internal struggle—he loved having a broader impact in the organization but missed the technical work. I leveraged the trusting relationship we had built to talk through the tough decision to move back to the technical ladder. I openly complimented Joel's courageous decision to follow his technical passion when announcing his move to the organization so it would not be perceived as a failure.

Eureka. I realized what makes me unique is my passion for motivating and getting people to their "best place" in their work life. This is another compelling aspect of my brand.

Oprah Winfrey has a strong and enviable brand. In the article published in the *Richmond Times Dispatch* on December 2, 2007, titled, "The O Factor," journalist Todd Boyd wrote:

> *She's in a category of her own. She's not a movie star.*
> *She's not a rock star. She's a brand. She's one of the*
> *few people in the world who can be identified only by*
> *one name. There's no question that Winfrey's status is*
> *unique. The Oprah Winfrey Show reaches close to*

nine million Americans each day. Then there's O, her
magazine, and her website. But she uses this personal
power for such good. Her philanthropy is well
publicized, especially the funding of her own school
for girls in South Africa.

Even Oprah's TV network is an extension of her brand. She is a powerhouse in leveraging that brand to accomplish the passion she has for helping others.

Invest the time to define your brand, and mine the gold from the journey to reveal what lights your fire.

THE STRENGTH TO FIND YOUR PASSION

Understanding what you're good at is the first step to defining your brand. As Apple is known for its intuitive user interface, your own brand clearly articulates what makes you different. Another aspect of my brand includes that of being a news reporter. I'm good at seeing the big picture unfolding and putting the spin on the story that summarizes the action.

The first time I remember using this news reporting intuition skill was while I was leading a huge development project. I saw tidbits of conversations and tension between team members that led me to believe we had a morale issue.

It's not enough to suspect there's an issue; a good leader finds out what's going on with her team. I like to take an unofficial poll by talking to individuals and asking how they think the group is doing.

Folks will usually tell you what's eating them when it's *in the name of the group*. No one wants to be singled out.

After gathering enough input to confirm and even tweak my intuition, I called the managers of the department together to share what I had learned in my one-on-ones with people. I was able to use my news reporting skills to summarize the situation, yet sprinkle in team anecdotes and stories I had heard to gain their buy-in to the problem. I sought their advice for addressing the burnout and was rewarded with some great suggestions for aggressively addressing the problem.

A great cowgirl recognizes the kick-ass impact her brand can make to the organization.

THE EXTROVERTED ENGINEER

Being a "wildfire" is another dimension of my brand. I am especially good at building excitement. In sales presentations, I'm good at painting a vision of where we move next. People invest in that vision. It's important to build a vision with authenticity. The vision has to be exciting not only in concept but with a high dose of we-could-really-get-there reality.

Being a wildfire has helped me to embrace the high-energy characteristic of my personality. In an R&D environment, that extroverted persona can be perceived as a liability, going with your gut, and not thoroughly thinking things through. This is understandable when getting as much data as possible is valued but can lead to analysis paralysis.

Being the wildfire in an introverted R&D ecosystem is like being that buffalo in the herd of cattle. Your difference shouldn't make you bad. Accept and celebrate what makes you different and unique. Leaning into your brand is as important to your success as it is for the cowgirl to understand and leverage the capabilities of her horse. A good cowgirl would never expect a bronco to be an exceptional show horse.

YOUR STRENGTH WILL SET YOU FREE

Finding your brand starts with getting clear about your strengths. One tool I use, Clifton's StrengthsFinder™, is from the book *Discover Your Strengths*. The book provides a code for readers to access the web-based survey that spits out your five strengths.

One of my strengths was WOO—winning others over. A WOO enjoys the challenge of meeting new people. Strangers are rarely intimidating to a WOO. On the contrary, strangers can be energizing. A WOO is drawn to them, wanting to learn their names, asking them questions to find some area of common interest to strike up a conversation and build rapport. Not only is a WOO rarely at a loss for words, he or she actually enjoys initiating interactions with strangers because the WOO derives satisfaction from breaking the ice and making a connection. In a WOO's world there are no strangers, only friends that haven't been met yet—lots of them.

I can't say that seeing WOO as one of my five strengths came as a total surprise. Learning how rare WOO is in an engineering environment helped me to better understand why I didn't quite fit in, and how this uniqueness could be leveraged in my brand.

Being a maximizer, a second strength, created additional opportunities for defining my brand. A maximizer derives satisfaction from taking something average and making it exceptional.

Once, my team burst into my office (as much as engineers can burst into an office) to tell me that they had fixed the system. They were so proud that it now only crashed once a day instead of every hour. I immediately asked if they were doing a root cause analysis to keep the system from ever crashing.

The deflated expressions on their faces confirmed the pitfall of being a maximizer. I was not satisfied with their average results, and my question demotivated them. This realization enabled me to begin responding differently to small achievements.

Leveraging your strengths only starts when you clearly understand them.

YOUR ENERGY METER: DRAIN OR INFUSE

Finding your passion is not only about identifying your strengths, but it's also about understanding what type of culture and environment unleashes your best self. Your job can either infuse energy into your life or suck you dry like the desert dust. Gain awareness of the energy drainers and energy infusers in your life. Keep a journal for a week, or just stop, breathe, and self-reflect. Are you revved up after giving a presentation or mentally tired? Does debugging a problem get your motor running or feel like sludge in your engine? Does attending a training class leave you spent? Find ways to do more of the activities that infuse energy in your life. If training leaves you flat, it doesn't mean you never attend another training course. It's about balance. You should be tipping the scales in favor of doing more energy-infusing activities in your workday.

Meeting new people and working together as a team infuse me with energy. One person's infuser can be another's drainer. If doing the detailed analysis for a problem pulls you down, there is probably another person on your team who finds this activity invigorating. This doesn't mean you never have to do those tasks that are energy drainers, but instead try to limit how many of these tasks you do in a day. Identify your energy infusers to improve your professional life and your happiness.

I was amazingly happy throughout my career in the high-tech engineering world. I was given all the leading, bleeding-edge projects to manage as a development director. I'll never forget finally finishing that eighteen-month, crazy-ass IP PBX project with one hundred twenty-five people in three countries and wondering what I could do next to top that.

But life's funny that way. When one door closes, a window opens. Little did I know that I would be a VP of Sales and Marketing of a software development company four short years later.

A COWGIRL ONLY GETS ONE CHANCE AT THIS LIFE

Some are blessed to know their passion from early in life. Most must do the hard work to discover theirs. Being fired after so many comfortable professional years was a blessing. I had a do-over, a chance to reinvent. A chance to get clear about my strengths, my brand, and my passion. It was a difficult journey, requiring tenacity and resilience. Out of despair and challenge comes clarity about your passion and what makes you fabulous. You will never be as successful as you could be until you find the work that you are passionate about.

I know few people who can say they are happy at their job and even fewer who can say they are passionate about their work. Passionate people say they feel excited about going to work on Monday morning. They can't believe they are paid for work they love. They feel they are living a bigger purpose with their life.

Managing people and making an impact in their lives connects me to that purpose. We aren't all called to cure cancer. Stand strong for finding that right work and place that allows you to be happy and successful because of who you are, not in spite of it. I wrote this book for you, so go out there and take your brand to heart.

CHAPTER SIX

VERSATILITY:
FROM BRONCO RIDER TO CALF ROPER

Wendy's Words

Take chances. Be extravagant in your career choices.

There's no way to be happy until you're on your divine right path.
Susan Taylor,* Essence *magazine editor

I asked my dad about trying out for the junior high basketball team. He enthusiastically replied, "Of course you should. You never know what you'll be good at." I later played college basketball on scholarship.

A great cowgirl is open to new opportunities and experiences. You never know what you'll discover you're good at. Most people suffer from a condition called life loss. That slow growing tumor where living your life gets in the way of having a life. My ninety-eight-year-old grandfather worked for Johns Manville from 1937 to 1977. My dad retired from AT&T at age fifty, after being hired right out of high school. Those days of finding your perfect job and retiring from there are over.

I've worked for seven different companies over my career. I've reinvented myself three times. From extroverted engineering director to sales executive to CEO of my own gender-intelligence consulting firm.

A career soul mate doesn't exist. Rethink your professional journey not as the search for the perfect job but instead a great ride through lots of great jobs. You may start your journey as a kick-ass rider, then learn that you are an even better calf roper.

REINVENTION (NOT NECESSITY) IS THE MOTHER OF INVENTION

Reinvention can be self-imposed or externally motivated. Being fired set me on my reinvention journey. But as the saying goes, "Cowgirl Up, or go sit in the truck." I decided to take six months to get my crap together and figure out what to do for the rest of my professional life. I spent the first two months trying to dig my way out of an all-time self-esteem low.

In hindsight, that time was necessary to come out of the valley of my life better. I learned from this experience that I couldn't hurry up the grieving process. I wish I had been more compassionate with myself. I learned that I was closer to being broken than I've ever been in my life—closer than when I lost my sixty-one-year-old dad to a massive heart attack a month after my daughter Madi was born.

My whole identity was wrapped up in that job. I recall driving home after packing my stuff in a cardboard box and being escorted out of the building, sobbing and heaving the whole way. I felt like the wife who drives up to her home and sees all her stuff piled up on the curb in the front yard, the only response from her husband of thirty years, "I don't love you anymore."

During that journey of reinventing myself, I took it out on the house. I repainted all the rooms in vibrant, rich colors. My husband, deeply connected with our white walls, was amazing with his support for my late-breaking decorating passion. I hadn't realized how much he and my family believed in me.

A month after I was fired, we went on a Caribbean cruise that had been planned for six months. I took my *I Was Fired and It's the Best Thing That Ever Happened to Me* book to keep me company. I wasn't the best traveling partner. My son and I met my daughter and husband in the local jewelry store after a day of excursions. My husband showed me this amazing big-ass diamond ring to replace my more sensible, we're-just-married and poor-as-dirt original stone. My engineer husband's typical response to previous suggestions of jewelry for a Christmas gift had been, "I've already given you jewelry. So that would be redundant."

I loved the new ring. Unlike other items, I believe size matters when it comes to diamonds. But, we had just lost 60 percent of our family income due to my firing. Now didn't seem the right time for big jewelry.

My husband told me he had planned to get me a bigger ring for our twentieth anniversary six months away. But it was what he then said that mattered more than the size of that new diamond. He said he knew I was destined for bigger and better things and this represented his faith in me. Out of the darkest moments of the cowgirl's journey come some of the brightest gifts, and I don't only mean diamonds.

After reinventing the house wearing my new big-ass ring, I moved on to the real work—me. I started the journey to figure out my next career move. I knew I didn't want to go back to another big company. More importantly, I started dreaming with no boundaries. I asked myself, and some trusted and respected friends, what I was good at. I was a maverick. Not afraid to talk to anyone. I loved being in the center of the chaos, taking on a cause to make things better. I loved networking and meeting new people. I was a natural connector.

I met a politician at a Rutgers's Women's Leadership retreat and was inspired. Why not politics? All these characteristics were valuable in a political career. I spent the next month investigating the profession by talking to every politician I could network with. Wisely I concluded that I am way too thin-skinned to live with the ugly personal attacks that come with the political territory. How cool to think outside the box about my next career move though!

WAITING FOR THE OTHER SHOE TO DROP

Four months into my six-month reinvention, a friend and CEO of a four-year-old software development start-up, pitched a job offer to me over a glass of wine. I wasn't ready to go back to work. I hadn't even started interviewing.

I still had healing to do, but opportunities rarely come at your preferred moments. They instead present themselves at mileposts in your life, lifting you out of your ordinary into the extraordinary.

The friend said she had been trying for two years to find a way to get me to join her in building the company. Here was someone who wanted me at my most needy time when I felt untouchable and abandoned by the company that had fired me.

She couldn't offer me the money I was making before, but she could offer me balance, a chance to help her grow the company to the next level, and a chance at partnership and company equity. The drawback was that they needed me now since they had a huge new data storage project.

I took some time to consider the offer. I was tentative about taking the job because I feared getting hurt again, loving a job and losing it. But they wanted me when the other company didn't. The CEO clinched the deal when she suggested I start the job while kicking off my job search. When asked why she would suggest such a crazy idea, she said, "Because you will love it so much here that you won't want to take a job with another company."

I negotiated starting immediately but working part-time for the remaining two months of my reinvention period. No sitting in the truck for me—time to Cowgirl Up!

During those first six months, people often asked me how I liked working at the new start-up. I responded, "It's good," in a tentative *hope-I-don't-jinx-it* voice. The little voice in my head continued to taunt me. *It will suck soon.* This could be referred to as fear of the other shoe dropping. Yet another opportunity to Cowgirl Up. Will they never end?

It took six full months for that little voice to stop. The healing happened at its own pace, but I hadn't let the fear own me. Cowgirling Up is most rewarding when you're most scared.

MOVING TO THE DARK SIDE

We all desire to find what we do in the world better than the average bear. When I was a new supervisor of a system test group, a wise female peer told me to find what each individual does better than most folks.

I had to look hard to discover what several of the folks in my group did best. Identifying others' strengths means taking the time to thoroughly get to know and understand people—a process that also builds positive rapport. I am never disappointed in how recognizing someone's strength lights him or her up.

In today's fast-paced world, few people take the time to build these types of relationships. It's worth the time since extraordinary things come out of strong relationships.

A boss took the time to notice my strength of building relationships with people. Meeting new people fascinates me, leading to my ultimate success as a salesperson. Within a few months of starting in the project manager role, I reached out to my personal network to see how we could help them with their development problems. At the time, I would never have called this being a salesperson. I grew up in the engineering world believing salespeople were slimy folks who couldn't tell the truth if their lives depended on it. Worse still, they sold things we didn't have, and made me figure out how to deliver them. The strongly held bias about sales prevented me from leaning into the role that was perfect for me as quickly as I could have. It's a sin not to lean into the gifts you have. I was sinning up a storm.

At my one-year performance review, the CEO asked me to do sales full time. I couldn't run from it any longer. I had to come to grips with my bias about sales people head on. After a large degree of internal debate, I realized I was meant to be a different type of salesperson: genuine, technical, and interested in helping customers solve their problems.

After taking the position, the first time someone asked me what I did, I covered my mouth and mumbled, "Sales and marketing." Cowgirl Up, Wendy. I never mumbled it again. Lean into your strengths like the amazing cowgirl leans into her wild bronco, grips the reins, and stays on.

COMING OUT OF THE EXTROVERTED CLOSET

Over the years in the male-dominated tech environment, I slowly took on a dimmer-switch approach to toning myself down. Then I discovered that most people actually respond positively to me being me. They like that I am direct and can lighten a tense situation with humor. They like that I give them crap and call them on theirs.

It is amazing that in a different position, such as sales, these same attributes can be viewed in an extremely different and positive light. It was as if I came out of the extrovert closet and was then accepted. People ask me how I survived being in engineering so long. It wasn't surviving. I prefer to think of it as the journey that led me to be the exact salesperson I was meant to be at this time in my career.

It's not what happens to you in your life journey, it's how you respond to it. Embrace struggles to make you better. It's not the horse you ride; it's how you ride the horse.

There will be many times in a cowgirl's professional life when her managers will not recognize the potential she possesses. In those moments, stay confident about what you have to offer.

A VP of Sales at a test company grew impatient at working below her level of competence. She was aware that her manager didn't know her skill set and what she could accomplish. Knowing she could make a bigger impact, she Cowgirled Up and put a slide deck together summarizing the company's business challenges and her action plan for attacking the issues. They loved her ideas and promoted her to director to implement the plan.

As her expertise grew in her new position, her dream job became clearer. She wanted to work for a Chief Operating Office (COO), help the company grow, and fix things. Leveraging the *power of intention*, she put what she wanted out in the universe.

Power of intention is similar to the power of prayer. You have to be careful what you ask for. The VP's clarity helped her obtain her next job. She ran into old acquaintances, owners of a very successful business. Later following up and sharing she was looking for a different job, they offered her a position to grow the commercial side of their business. When the CEO described the new position, he used the exact words she used when she described her perfect job. Uncanny!

START-UP COWGIRL OR CORPORATE COWGIRL?

What if your perfect position is leading a business? How do you decide if you're destined to be a business owner or a part of a big corporation? When asked why Carol Bartz, executive chairman of software maker Autodesk, never left the corporate world, she said, "It would never have dawned on me to set up my own company. Ever. I am much more interested in the give-and-take of a large organization... I don't think it's as simple as saying that women are frustrated and off they go. When that happened to me, I found another company. It's how I'm wired" (Lanpher 2007, 57).

Margaret Heffernan has launched three companies. She has a slightly different take. In her words, "The heart of the question is, how come some women stay and slug it out, and others think, to heck with this, I'm out of here? For my part, I stayed at one organization for thirteen years quite happily. And then came a moment when I thought, I can't do this anymore" (Lanpher 2007, 59).

One approach to answering this question is to do some introspection to see if you're an entrepreneur at heart. Do you love to innovate? Are there departments in your company where this attribute is a prerequisite? Some product companies have research teams chartered to discover product innovation ideas. For those companies that don't have these opportunities, you may be forced to build your own ladder.

It's important to identify what's holding you back from your perfect position. For a former team member of mine, being a *thermometer* was holding her back. If those around her were happy, she was happy. If they were bitching and dissatisfied with a situation, she was negative. You have the ability to decide how you will respond to a situation. You can add to the dysfunction or be the light out of it. It's your choice. You can be bucked off or last that full eight seconds.

THE COWGIRL'S NEXT ACT

A 2015 report by American Institute for Economic Research (AIER) found that 82 percent of people forty-seven and older who tried to transition to new careers in the two previous years were successful

(Rosato 2015). If those of us with more miles on our tires can reinvent ourselves, surely the young whippersnappers can. Never get stagnant. Be open to new experiences. Be learning and looking for what lights your fire.

Your sweet spot is the intersection between what you already know, what you're good at, and what you love doing. It's what you jump out of bed for in the morning and stay up for late at night. What's holding you back? What positives would happen if you took the leap? When your work reflects your passion, you wake up excited. Two of the most important days in your life are the day you were born and the day you found out why. You owe it to the world and yourself to not settle for what you could do but instead fight to find out what you should do. Reinvent yourself cowgirl!

.

CHAPTER SEVEN

SPEAKING THE LANGUAGE OF THE COWBOYS

Wendy's Words

You can be right or you can be effective.

It's not what you say. It's how you say it.

The limits of my language mean the limits of my world.

Ludwig Wittgenstein

"Time is money, y'all." My development team heard this consistently throughout the life of a project. It was my way of reinforcing the need to weigh schedule versus quality versus functionality.

When developing a product, you can get two of these three but never all three. Your credibility as a leader is directly proportional to how well your team delivers on schedule. My reputation as the head of a leading-edge R&D team was dependent on understanding, to the core of my being, this two-out-of-three concept. When I say understand it, I mean the way a cowgirl understands small changes in pressure on her reins can get her horse to change directions immediately.

Knowing the language of your industry means not only knowing your stuff technically, but also communicating differently based on your audience. Success is directly related to how well you speak the language of the cowboys in both content and delivery.

Authenticity in communication portrays strength in what you say. I can tell when my direct reports answer a question with suspect information. I call this "eye patching."

When she was thirteen, my daughter gave an eloquent explanation for why pirates wear eye patches, spinning a unique tall tale that they spend so much time below deck that the eye patch helps them adjust their eyes more slowly as they come up on the main deck.

I was sincerely impressed with the passion in which she spoke to the point, but when I asked her where she got the information, its lack of validity was exposed.

Eye patching is easy to resort to since most of us despise the feeling of not knowing something. However, it is not authentic, and you lose precious credibility when you *eye patch*. A confident cowgirl commits to confirming the answer to a question she's not certain of, and follows up 100 percent of the time.

Growing up in Virginia shaped the colloquialisms I use. Like cultures, different industries (e.g., finance, technology, manufacturing, etc.) have their own unique languages and local accents. Using words like *y'all* makes me wonder if maintaining my Southern accent actually harmed my career. People's first impressions of you stick. Unfortunately, Southerners are sometimes stereotyped as slow and not the sharpest knives in the drawer. Once I interviewed with the CEO at a technology company. Things seems to be going well, when he stopped the interview and abruptly said, "I have to admit, I wasn't sure about you when you first came in, but I'm really impressed with you. You're so intelligent and articulate and so perceptive about how we can grow the business."

It was like one of those backhanded compliments, "You rope pretty well for a girl." I wondered if my Southern accent led him to his first impression of me since I hadn't spoken or dressed outrageously. I thanked him but spent the rest of the interview looking for confirmation of full sexist credentials, like a cowgirl sizing up the bronco she's going to ride.

I weighed the typecasting my Southern accent might bring and decided being myself was a risk I would take. I mitigated the risk of being perceived as not as smart by making sure I knew my stuff. I've always worked harder to be prepared and be continuously learning.

Speaking the language of the cowboys will help you be your most successful only if you're able to be your authentic self.

IT'S NOT THE TITLE, IT'S THE CREDIBILITY

I've noticed that people judged me differently as a sales VP than they did as an R&D director. As Southerners can be judged as not the sharpest knife, pretty sales VPs may suffer the same prejudice. I've seen the mental shift in a prospect's eyes after I started asking detailed, technical follow-up questions.

I found it quickened the process to let slip that I was an extroverted engineer who had worked as one of the few R&D women directors. (You figure out ways to mention your credentials in passing since women aren't supposed to boast.)

One fellow actually said, "Wow, you'll be able to get this then," after I asked why they decided to spend the R&D dollars to implement SIP instead of H.323 in their solution. Knowing your stuff earns credibility, a precious commodity in the business world.

How does a cowgirl go about acquiring the ability to speak the language? With an intention equal to that of learning how to rope a steer, a woman must listen and pick up the unique language of their industry. One of the quickest ways to do this is to listen carefully to those you respect. Follow the blog of thought leaders in your industry, and pay attention to not only content but also how their blogs are written. What slang do they use? Make sure to follow both female and male thought leaders. Follow them on twitter to stay current with the information they find relevant. If industry leaders are talking about something you don't know about, learn about it.

FAKE IT TILL YOU MAKE IT

Those of us working our way up the high-tech professional ladder must conquer terms like *Big Data*, *Web 2.0*, and *WIMAX*. When I say conquer, I mean these words and phrases must roll off the tongue with absolute confidence. For a technical cowgirl, this becomes ever more important.

As a reader at my church, I am often perplexed by the pronunciation of the more obscure biblical city names. My pastor's advice to me applies inside my church as well as inside my office. I am to say the words confidently without any degree of hesitancy.

Profound business advice. Even when you are still learning, stretch yourself to use the language. Claim it as your own—practicing until you are comfortable using it. Much like most things in life, practice makes perfect.

The importance of credibly speaking the language can be found at the auto mechanic's shop. Think back to the last time you had your car serviced. Did you understand the words your mechanic used to describe the services offered? I now think of this type of exchange as a game I have to play whenever I get my car serviced. Before going, I network with my car-savvy friends to acquire the language to speak intelligently with the service technician.

If the technician says the fuel pump needs to be replaced and I don't have a clue what the fuel pump does, I ask questions until I am sure my car's symptoms match the technician's diagnosis.

We have all heard the stories about women who pay for services not required because they can't decipher the language the technicians use. Likewise, in a business setting, asking questions and deferring decisions until all knowledge is obtained surely increases a woman's success.

Every trade and industry has a specific language for communicating. In the high-tech industry, we have a language as well as an ever-changing list of acronyms. Some examples are: TCP/IP (Transmission Control Protocol/Internet Protocol), ADSL (Asymmetric Digital Subscriber Line), LAN (Local Area Network), and SIP (Session Initiated Protocol).

It's been my experience that many folks start using acronyms without first finding out what the letters represent. In fact, some acronyms are so familiar and used so frequently few remember what they stand for—such as laser or IBM.

Once I met with a couple of social media consultants to investigate better online visibility for our company. One spoke using the latest hot social terms while the other lacked the same ease of the language. If a person does not confidently incorporate acronyms specific to her industry, she is at a business disadvantage.

WE'RE ONLY AS GOOD
AS OUR LAB NOTEBOOK

I remember my first day at my first job. Their corporate complex was an assortment of impressively massive buildings where it was quicker to hop the shuttle bus between buildings than walk the country mile to my car and drive over for meetings.

Now imagine me as a young, fresh graduate. I was a rather naïve, young Southern woman when I showed up for my first real product meeting. I was excited and determined to jump right in and show off my college degree. What a shock I had when in those first five minutes of my first meeting, I was bombarded with acronyms.

Instead of contributing to the meeting, I spent most of my time jotting all the words and acronyms down in my newly acquired *Lab Notebook*. Years later, I am still scribbling all the impressive things I learn every day in a cuter notebook in my endless quest to keep up with the language of technology. Just goes to show you how much the tech industry continues to evolve. My entries are a virtual timeline of the technologies I have been exposed to over the course of my career.

That first meeting taught me an important life lesson. I didn't have all the answers, and to be successful, I'd have to embrace that I was always learning.

Tracking down definitions and the meaning of acronyms was not what I imagined I'd be doing on a regular basis at my job. At first I had to muster the courage to admit I didn't know the language or the meaning of their acronyms. I learned that folks didn't expect me to already know it, but they did expect me to be quick about getting up to speed. I began acquiring the IT language with the comforting understanding that my peers and those above me were on similar journeys.

Knowing what you don't know is the first step in gaining power through language.

THE POWER OF THE ACRONYM

Another quirky part of the tech culture is seen in the attention given to project names. A typical beginning of every new bleeding-edge project involves the creation of a catchy code name. At most project kickoff meetings, "Let's name the project" is a separate agenda item. There is actually a method to the madness.

The project code name must be powerful and catchy, like C-Hawk, never Goldfish. There will always be one engineer in the crowd who suggests an acronym that is less than appropriate for the six-and-under crowd, generally a name like Asynchronous Static Systems (ASS). Stifling the R-rated definitions quickly with a stern but amused don't-make-me-come-over-there mommy-look was an effective technique I used to corral all the crazy ideas and to keep the fun above the belt. The people who create the project names are actually the people in power. Furthermore, if you don't know what the C-Hawk project is, then you're out of *the know*. Those who have the inside information about the C-Hawk project are the in-crowd, those folks inside the circle of trust.

My reputation expanded or diminished depending upon my ability to bring up the latest and greatest project code names in water cooler conversations. I gained valuable power points by being in the know. Silly? Yes, but true. With power comes a fair amount of respect and credibility. Pay attention to the project code names, acronyms, and language shifts. Language is power.

SOME OF MY BEST FRIENDS ARE GEEKS

The speed at which you acquire the knowledge can make or break you as a female bronco rider or an aspiring businesswoman. Years into my career, I jumped into an area I knew nothing about—becoming the manager of the company's new VoIP development group.

I was known as a telephony gal, not as a router/data switch guru. But I didn't let this sway me. I took the bull by the horns, humbled myself, and asked a particularly empathetic technical *geek* for assistance. I say *geek* here in the most loving and respectable manner as I have a wide circle of geek friends and colleagues whom I respect and truly appreciate. I digress. Back to my story about how I evolved into a router/data switch guru.

For about two weeks after taking on my new assignment, I spent several hours each day drinking from a fire hose to get the basics. It was intimidating and time consuming but invaluable. By developing a foundational understanding, I was able to ask credible questions, gather the information to make informed decisions, and gain respect from my team. Knowing what you don't know and being brave enough to aggressively fill the knowledge gap is important.

A few years ago, I spoke at the Voice on the Net (VON) conference. My ability to speak the telecom language fluently paid off during this experience. VON was the definitive VoIP event of the year.

The conference had more than a decade of history delivering exceptional networking and learning experiences to wire line, wireless, and broadband IP communications C-level (i.e., CEO, CTO, COO) attendees. At this four-day event, key people from around the world gathered to launch new products, listen to industry-savvy speakers, and learn from the experts. And I was invited to speak.

At the conference, I walked into the hotel bar for my first prep meeting with our public relations (PR) staff about the media interviews I would support. As I chatted with the various sales and PR folks, a particularly outgoing marketing woman asked me a rather blunt question. "How did you get so technical?"

I wondered what she meant. Were women not supposed to be technical? Was she complimenting me or putting me down? I felt my femininity being challenged. I couldn't put my finger on why her question had unnerved me. So without knowing how to respond, I said what came to my mind first, "Working in research and development for decades does that to a person."

Her response indicated she was impressed with my high-tech know-how. Yet another life lesson that having the technical knowledge was table stakes in my industry.

What did I do that gave her the impression that I was technical? I definitely didn't write any call management code on a cocktail napkin while I was sipping my drink. What did I say that allowed her to see me as a competent technical person? It was due to the acronyms and the language I used to discuss the project. When the SIP topic came up, I was able to add content and detail concerning the subject since I was the development director for our initial SIP offer.

Speaking in a definitive manner on a subject can be foreign to some women. For me it goes back to my upbringing. Comments like "pretty is as pretty does" and "don't be so full of yourself" were common. Knowing what you're good at is the definition of being full of yourself. In the business world, being full of yourself is exactly what allows you to present that confident demeanor to let people know, "I'm the right person to manage that $34 million development project."

A LITTLE KNOWLEDGE CAN BE A DANGEROUS THING

When I acquired responsibility to build the SIP solution for our portfolio, I didn't know SIP from SAP (Systems, Applications, and Products). I quickly learned enough about SIP to get *cowgirl* dangerous. In the technical environment, this is called speed learning. It's like drinking from a fire hose, definitely not "SIPping" from a fire hose (little techy humor again).

Speed learning allows you to hold your own in a technical discussion so people can't pull the wool over your eyes or snow you. You don't have to know how to debug the SIP messages from the output of a sniffer, but you must know the subject in enough detail to be able to do your job.

Speed learning also enables you to quickly assess project issues to either remove barriers for the team and/or give feedback about the approach to the issue. Being a fast learner is one of the most important skills I leveraged consistently throughout my career. My quick mastery of the language has been a tremendous asset to speaking the language of the technology cowboys.

My ability to speak the language also allowed me to be a confident panelist at the IP PBX Showdown. This industry competition had representatives seated across the stage in front of five hundred people. I was the only woman on the panel and less than 10 percent of the audience was women.

I couldn't help but see the word *showdown* as a perfect example of the masculine energy projected in the event. Showdown conjures up images of two mean, rather dirty cowboys, squaring off at the O.K. Corral to see who's left standing. Not the typical approach most women take to solving a business problem, would you say?

The IP PBX Showdown event was a highly anticipated annual event pitting industry competitors against each other in a most obvious way. It was all about delivering the verbal knockout punch.

I was seated beside our top competitor. Each panelist was required to provide an overview of their architecture, advantages of their solution, and cost savings availed in only two minutes. This was the first test of the event—talking fast. I'm good at that.

After all panelists presented their two-minute overviews, we asked each other questions to illuminate solution weaknesses. Since I was scheduled to pose the first question, I could set the tone for the event by throwing the proverbial first punch.

Having heard of our competitor's tendency to go on the offensive early, I intended to beat them to the punch with my own unique style. I've learned over the years that you can actually say practically anything ugly with a smile and get away with it. I won't deny that the charm that goes along with the Southern accent has aided me with this maneuver. Speaking directly can create enough uncertainly to catch the intended off-balance. I have used this approach strategically over the years to let others know I won't be pushed around or talked down to.

Having done my homework prior to the Showdown event, I had prepared two very compelling drawbacks to our competitor's solution. In terms of the VoIP market-share war, their offer achieved the early jump in the market. But we got back in the game and took market-share leadership through some very innovative solutions. I was lucky enough to lead the team responsible for one of the solutions.

THE ONE-TWO PUNCH

My first question to the panelist challenged the claim that their solution was easy to manage. I led with a typical three-thousand-agent contact center scenario and set up the question by stating that their solution required sixty-four servers whereas our solution required only two. I asked how they could claim ease of management with so many more servers. The panelist rambled on about how their management system made the number of servers transparent to the user, blah, blah,

blah. I would have loved to have yelled *not* at this point to call him on his bluff, but sanity prevailed. As the next panelist asked his question, the panelist I had zinged leaned over and whispered to me, "I knew you would ask the number of servers question."

I quickly countered, "Bet you five bucks you don't see the next one coming."

Throughout my life I have always felt slow in providing the ever-elusive comeback. I don't think I have ever been prouder of my quick wit. Credibility is not only built through the selection of words but the attitude with which you say them.

My favorite portion of the debate was questioning the panelist about an obvious outage in their offer. I asked politely how their SIP phone in our SIP solution supports fourteen of the SIPPING seventeen standard features, whereas the SIP phone in their own solution only supports four. I ended the question with, "It seems that we work with your solution better than you work with your own solution."

My mamma taught me not to revel in other people's misfortunes, but I would be lying if I did not own up to a degree of satisfaction in watching the guy squirm. It was all I could do not to pump my fist in the air and yell a triumphant "Yahoo!" in victory. Doing my homework had never been so rewarding!

Even more interesting to me was one of the other panelist's feedback at the conclusion of the event. "Well, aren't you the little wolf in sheep's clothing." Having said it with a smile instead of a smirk, I timidly responded with a feeble thank-you.

I wish I had not been so caught up in the win to take the time to ask him whether this was a compliment or slam. The comment would never have been targeted to a man. I took the statement as his way of complimenting me because I played the game like a man.

It was as if the panelist was saying, Aren't you a boy in girl's clothing. It made me reflect upon my approach to sports in college. I wanted to look like a girl but play like a boy. I wore school-color coordinating ribbons around my ponytail while kicking some butt on the basketball court.

I was doing the exact same thing now in the male-dominated high-tech industry. I was dressing like a girl and acting as aggressively as a man. The ability to fluently talk *the* language with confidence and the substance to back it up is imperative to being successful in the workplace and in life. It never hurts to make sure you look good doing it.

YOU CAN BE RIGHT OR YOU CAN BE EFFECTIVE

Women are expected to speak differently than men. Men and even some women have less tolerance for abrupt, direct questions or statements. We're considered a bitch if we get right to the point. It feels like this comes from the expectation of women as nurturers.

Have you ever noticed how men can have a knock-down, drag-out fight in a technical discussion and then walk away talking about where they are going to lunch? Women tend to hold on to grudges so much longer. Different genders have different expectations for how we speak.

"I thought you said you would take care of this? Right?" The e-mail question seemed harmless. I was asking a peer why I was getting another e-mail from accounting after he said he would take care of the situation.

His response, "Really no need to act like that, Wendy, it's not a good way to start your week off," was unprofessional and rude.

Men expect women to not be direct, to ease into a request or question. I suppose a more nurturing e-mail might have read, "Hope your day is off to a good start. Hey, got an e-mail from accounting asking again about those expenses. You had mentioned you would work with them on it several weeks ago. I'm sure you've been busy, but could you let me know when you will have a completion date?"

Having to water down our communication is not fair. Cowgirls must learn how to succeed in the business world that we find ourselves. It's not what you say; it's how you say it. Men aren't as strictly held to this rule. But cowgirls, you can be right, or you can be effective. So to be effective (and successful) in the workplace, consider how you phrase your words, as well as being extremely knowledgeable of the content.

When we're in charge, we can change the culture to ensure being direct is appreciated regardless of what gender delivers the message.

I THINK I CAN, I THINK I CAN

Someone once gave me advice about sharing my opinion. If you want people to know how smart you are and risk having them disagree with you, use the word *think*. Think refers to the things you know in your head.

When you want people to know your message is coming from your core and is based upon your values and set of beliefs, use the word *believe.*

Positioning in this way lets people "hear" you and listen versus look for ways to contradict you. I'm not saying you should band the phrase *I think* from your vocabulary. Become aware of how often you're using the phrase, and tweak your speech accordingly to use *I believe* instead.

TIMING IS EVERYTHING

It's not only how you phrase the words but also choosing the right moment to say them. Timing is as important as knowing the language. Comedy depends on timing. Pausing before the punch line can make or break a joke.

A great product manager I worked with, Tom Cornelius, tickled me with his lighthearted approach to getting engineers to stop what they were doing to answer his question. "Put your screwdrivers down." They made time for him every time.

As a teenager, rehashing a date with my mom usually ended with her saying, "What you should have said…" Over the years, I've developed the timing skill to say the right thing at the right moment. It was responsible for my success at the VON IP PBX Showdown. Timing can make or break a sale. Is now the right time to ask for the close? Asking too early can be disastrous to the deal. The calf roper must trust her gut to pick the exact right moment to jump off her horse.

LASSOING THE LANGUAGE

Knowing the language of your industry leads to your success. It's usually difficult but not impossible to conquer. Cowgirl Up. Do what it takes, leveraging every resource available to gain that knowledge.

Use the language with attitude and intention. Speak with confidence—head held high and looking directly into their eyes. Be intentional about choosing the right timing for the ask. Remember, it's as important the way you say something as what you say.

Language gives you power. Use it wisely, Grasshopper.

CHAPTER EIGHT

NETWORKING IS ROPIN' THEM IN

Wendy's Words

The secret to networking is an innate fascination in people.

Networking is an essential part of building wealth.
Armstrong Williams

On the range, a good cowgirl knows her way around a rope. She scans the herd, sees the right horse, and aggressively swings her lasso over the horse's neck. Her business begins with that first contact. She now starts the dance of ropin' them in. This is how it works with a networking relationship. Once you spot someone you're interested in doing business with, networking is making the connection and ropin' them in.

Ben Casnocha, author of *My Start-Up Life*, used this ropin' analogy. He writes, "How do you get an 'A' player to work with you? Court them smartly" (Casnocha 2007, 78).

Casnocha shares how he built relationships with advisory board members of his first company, Comgate, his start-up company aimed at linking the community with local government. He started with a simple contact and then spent years ropin' them in until they had psychologically committed to the company on a deep level.

Making the *ask* before the relationship is established can kill the deal. Casnocha says it is not easy to rope someone in, and that, "Courtship takes time, dedicated focus on the real 'A' players, and an awareness of the individual's psychological disposition" (Casnocha 2007, 79).

Casnocha was phenomenal because he not only had to run board meetings for Comgate—the business he started at age twelve as a project for his sixth-grade tech class—but he had to also find time to attend high school. If a high school senior can network to build his business, we as competent older and wiser professionals have no excuse.

The secret to being a good networker lies in an innate fascination in other people. I have interviewed a herd of people during the creation of this book. They had depth, passion for what they were doing or the journey they were on, and a strong likeability factor. I enjoyed spending time with them.

As the rancher meticulously scrutinizes each horse in the auction to find the right addition to her herd, you must approach each person you meet with curiosity and discover his or her inner wealth. It's easier to find than you think, and as they say, the journey is most of the adventure.

NETWORK BEFORE YOU NEED IT

The worst time to start building your network is when you need it. Kristin Russell, president of Arrow Electronics, is one of the most genuinely compassionate leaders I've met and a world-class networker. Kristin offers, "Always have a keen interest in maintaining relationships since you don't know when you're going to need people. People are shortsighted about building a network. The time to build a network is before you need it. It's awesome when a contact you've built a relationship with calls later and says there's this job and I thought about you."

THE ASKING IS EASY

Dipping into someone else's web of established relationships is the truest definition of networking. I call this connectional networking, one of three types of networking.

I'll never forget trying to rope in my first mentor. It seemed weird. Do you walk up to someone you admire and ask him or her to be your mentor, like you'd ask a cute boy to the Sadie Hawkins dance?

I used connectional networking and asked my favorite manager whom he would recommend and had him provide the introduction. This approach is easiest since it leverages the relationship you have with someone you already trust and dips into that person's network. I respected my manager's opinion so it was a safe bet to assume whomever he chose would be a good fit.

Opportunities present themselves weekly to connect someone I meet to someone in my network. I am a natural connector. I recently met a fabulous chemical engineer with an innovative product improving safety in the refinery industry. She had been asked to consider an associate dean position at a local prestigious university. Understanding how overwhelming a career leap like this might be, I offered to introduce her to a female dean who had made a similar move from business to academia.

Building value by connecting people only builds your own impact currency. It feels good when you help another cowgirl or cowboy out.

The second, but most frequent and effective approach, is called relational networking. Allowing a relationship to develop over time creates a deeper connection. Ben Casnocha learned this networking technique at a very young age.

I still feel deeply connected to one of my first mentors, who exemplified commitment to my success by telling me the hard stuff. He said, "Wendy, you have to get used to people not liking you if you're ever going to be successful. You're a pleaser."

A cowgirl's success grows as her relationship with her horse grows and deepens over time. Most greenhorn networkers walk into an industry event, collecting business cards like bullets on a gun belt. An experienced cowgirl knows it's quality of networking that matters, not quantity.

The third approach, situational networking, leverages your network to solve a problem or achieve a specific goal. You're in the middle of an issue or challenge and need some advice or insight on how to move forward.

No one knows the importance of situational networking more than Praful Shah who has invested in over fifty companies since 2008, half of them with women founders or CEOs. A successful male angel investor, Praful suggests, "It's most important to take advice from someone you trust and who has been successful in that arena. I see a lot of people getting advice from the wrong people. If it's investment advice you need, ask them how many companies have they invested in. We have a saying in India originating from how women carry water on their heads— *'Half-empty vessel swooshes more.'*"

Sadly, the less knowledgeable people tend to give the most advice and make the most noise. Finding the right expert is the key to being a killer situational networker.

Cowgirl Up! Networking		
Type	**Why**	**How**
Relational	Build your network organically	Relationship develops over time into a valued member of your network.
Situational	Build your network due to a specific situation or goal	Leverage your network to solve a problem or challenge.
Connectional	Build value by connecting members within your network	Providing worth to your network by connecting others while increasing your impact currency.

All three of these networking approaches work. Your success comes from choosing the approach you're most comfortable with and best fits the circumstance. A cowgirl picks her roping partner carefully.

MENTORING 101

Once you've networked to find that right mentor, here are some simple tips for making the most of the opportunity.

1. As a mentee, first introduce yourself by providing your name, your role in the company, and a brief summary of your business experience.
2. Ask your mentor for her/his current role and a brief work history. Take notes.
3. Agree to confidentiality; trust is the basis of every relationship.
4. Discuss a current challenge to break the ice. Describe the context and the situation with enough detail so your mentor can provide insightful advice, but not so much that you bore them with too much information. Be open and listen.
5. Before completing your conversation, determine an action that moves you forward.
6. Report on your efforts at solving the problem in a timely manner.
7. Finally, it's best to schedule the next meeting before you end the current one, as mentors are usually busy people.

Use these tips to develop the new relationship. Your mentor will be impressed with the intention you bring. You will be building a partnership where you can reach out when things get tough or you could use a sounding board.

MENTORS TELL YOU THE HARD STUFF

After two years at a software solution company, I noticed an opportunity that seemed out of reach. I had been working in a sales hunter role for a year and a half, and although I was good at it, it wasn't meeting my deeper need to build something bigger and more lasting. I threw my hat into the ring as the CEO of the healthcare spinoff company we were investing in.

When I presented the proposal to the chairman of the board, I felt like I was a little girl playing dress-up. What made me think I could be a CEO?

I needed the adrenaline hit that a conversation with my mentor could provide. Not because she would agree with me, but because she would give me honest feedback about what I needed to be an exceptional CEO candidate. Mentors and trusted advisors do that. They provide the gift of genuine feedback.

Mentorships require an investment of time, both yours and theirs. With any good relationship, both parties gain. It's like your momma told you, "Having a good friend means being a good friend." How can you give back to your mentor? Perhaps the energy rush she gets from seeing you at a gutsy part of your career is all the mentor needs. But why not ask her how you can support or help her? I offered to introduce a mentor to someone in a similar consulting firm role that I felt she would hit it off with. Both were so pleased to have found each other.

Having a good mentor means being a good mentor. What cowgirl would get in the ring without her rodeo clowns?

WHAT HAVE YOU DONE FOR ME LATELY?

It seems as women rise up the corporate ladder they sometimes become less willing to mentor others. This has been called "C-snobbery," the belief that a C-level is too busy and her time is too precious to mentor. Cow pies! How the heck did C-levels get to their high rank? By others mentoring them.

Kristin Russell shares why she mentors, "I never approach networking as asking for something for myself. Being intentional and interested in how I can help others has been the key to building my network. Once a relationship is established, others have always been there for me. I've learned so much from those I've helped. People reach out to me every week, inquiring if I know anyone who might be able to help them. The strength of my network allows me to help in almost every case. It's our responsibility as women who have made it to be there for each other."

What legacy are you leaving? Mentoring others will help you grow as much as your mentee.

YOU HAVE TO GIVE TO GET

What are the keys to growing a relationship? It's all a palms' up approach; it is not a handout, what-are-you-going-to-do-for-me approach. For example, I was checking out the "answers" section of

LinkedIn, the ever-popular professional networking website, and I saw a request for a recommendation of a company to run a virtual focus group. I had met the CEO of an innovative company called User Centric on a recent business trip to Chicago. I had been impressed with the CEO and the company, so I called my new User Centric CEO contact to ask if it was okay to recommend them. I then responded to the request with a recommendation and included the CEO's contact info on the site. He was blown away that I thought of them. This is artfully ropin' them in.

I recall when a friend told me, "You've got to meet Roxanne." Listen up when people you respect want to introduce you to someone. Roxanne is my professional identical twin. Her career journey paralleled my own. After getting laid off from a two-decade career at Qwest, she allowed herself two months to network for her next position. Her motto during these self-reflective months was "Give before you get." She researched two leading-edge technology topics, RFID and VoIP-enabled Web Services, and created a PowerPoint that she would share with people over those two months. She wanted them to get something out of their time with her. This was a creative and effective way for her to fulfill her intention to give as much as you can during her transition. Her ideas inspired me to be creative in developing my own networking style.

NOT EVERYONE IS WORTH A LUNCH

As a novice networker, I scheduled a weekly Friday appointment reminding me to contact two business associates I hadn't talked with in a while. As I matured in my skills as a world-class networker, I enhanced my technique by entering a recurring appointment for every person I wanted to stay connected with. For each of these appointments, I either set up a phone conference or invited them for coffee, a beer, or a meal.

But as Annette Quintana, owner of Istonish Holding Company, commented in her own direct and captivating style, "Not everyone is worth a lunch." This could be taken as a bit cold and calculated, but you only have so much time to invest in these networking relationships.

As you strategize investment in a retirement account, you also must strategize how to invest your time networking. Pick a reasonable goal for how much time you'll spend, similar to setting a percentage of your take-home for your company's 401k. I suggest one event a week (either over lunch or after hours) such as a tech meetup group or an industry event. Work up to it. Ramp up too quickly or pick a too aggressive goal, and you'll burn out and stop all together. Every cowgirl doesn't compete in every rodeo.

Bill Hoberecht, owner of Pinnacle Performance, a project management consulting shop, has a unique take on how he incorporates networking into his overcrowded schedule. He blocks out every Tuesday from ten a.m. to two p.m. to do coffee, lunch, coffee, and then e-mail. This time is specifically focused on increasing his network.

He targets three groups of people to touch:

1. Executives who he wants to connect with on an ongoing basis,

2. Folks who are in his functional area of expertise (i.e., project managers or even competitive companies), and

3. Renegades, people who others he respects have suggested he get to know.

Bill created the time to network in his day because it was important to his success.

Finding the time to exercise is much like finding the time to network. I have to exercise first thing in the morning before the day gets totally out of control. Much like exercise, the more you network, the more it becomes second nature. What cowgirl skips a day of riding her horse?

I'M GETTING PAID TO TALK

Networking usually comes more easily to extroverts than introverts. Ask introverts how they feel after talking to clients all day at a conference. They are wiped! As a flaming extrovert, the closest I've come to this feeling was at my first industry conference. I checked in with my husband, midday of the first day of the conference, to provide commentary on my new sales role. I summarized my role as "I'm being paid to talk."

Always quick-witted, he responded, "Too bad they're not paying you by the word, we'd be rich." I barely had the energy at the end of the day to call home to say good night to my family. Even I was tired of talking. My natural skills were stretched to their limit.

As you exercise to strengthen your muscles, you must continually stretch to do things you're uncomfortable with. Strengthen your networking muscles. Try these ideas. Talk to the stranger sitting next to you on the plane. Strike up a conversation with the person in front of you in the Starbucks line. Every opportunity to be with people may lead to networking. To be successful, introverts must network with a purpose. Treat networking like you would a shopping trip with a limited amount of money in your pocket. Spend it wisely.

NETWORK TO FIND THE RIGHT NETWORK

Both extroverts and introverts will be more effective by planning networking like it's work to get done. You go out to the barn to ride the horse. To ride, you need a horse. If you don't have one, find someone who knows all about horses so you can get the right one for you.

Don't network to gather business cards. Find the right people to help you and your business. For example, say your business needs to grow a new healthcare vertical. Touch as many people to find those most knowledgeable about the healthcare industry. Who are the movers and shakers in the industry?

Brendan Reidy, CEO of Clarus, a software company out of San Francisco, once told me, "The telecom industry is really the same small group of fifty people, and you keep running into them as they move and shift jobs."

Networking starts with finding out who are those fifty most influential people in your industry. Riding starts with the right horse.

NETWORKING 101

You've identified someone you'd like to meet. How do you network? With a smile on your face (important since who would ever want to talk with a crabby pus), walk up to him, introduce yourself, and ask him what he does. Then continue to ask questions to dig deeper, hang on his words like he is the most interesting person you've ever talked with. At first you might have to fake the interest part, but as the saying goes, "Fake it till you make it." Soon you'll be excited about how interesting people are.

Once you've captivatingly learned about a potential new contact, go back and write down the highlights. I usually jot them in the notes section of my Microsoft Outlook contact for that person. And not merely the professional stuff, like they make all the outsourcing decisions for the company. I also record personal information, such as the names of their spouse and children, where they went to school, interests that they mentioned. Do they like to hike? Were they in Hawaii for their last vacation?

This all must come from a place of genuine interest. If you don't feel engaged at first, fake it till you make it. Trust me. You will become interested once you use your first fascinating tidbit.

Knowing the little-known, nonprofessional facts about people shows your softer side. Think back to the great boyfriend who remembered you liked vanilla and brought you over a Starbucks vanilla latte the last time he dropped by. You felt special, right? He went to the trouble of remembering what you liked. Knowing your client is your job as a networker. Know your horse.

Oh my gosh, I'm a Hallmark card. I make network-because-you-care moments. A couple of years ago, I met this incredibly smart engineer with a passion for origami. When I visited his office, I noticed his fabulous collection. Later, I sent him an article about origami. I put a sticky note on it that said, "Thought you would like this." His response was what made the event memorable. He called and told me how much it meant to him that I had remembered.

IT'S THE THOUGHT THAT COUNTS

Another effective tip is, when you discover a client's or peer's birthday, put it on your calendar so you can send them a card, quick e-mail, or text on their next birthday. It goes back to the golden rule, "Do unto others as you would have them do unto you."

People love when you remember their children. Is your client's child into the theatre? Leave him or her a quick message about an upcoming seminar for budding actors. Networking is showing someone you're interested in him or her professionally and as a person. Be creative in how you network by being informed.

USE TECHNOLOGY FOR GOOD NOT EVIL

I've come up with a couple of reliable methods to leverage technology and network more effectively:

1. Keep note files in Microsoft Outlook for recurring trips, (i.e. "Next Dallas Trip" might include a list of the folks you should try to see while you're there). This is different from searching your Outlook contacts to find everyone who lives in Dallas. This prioritizes who is "worth" seeing during your next busy business trip. *Because* you're flying in from out of town, people will make time to see you. *Use it.*

2. Record in your Outlook Contact an ongoing summary of the highlights from each meeting: topics discussed and any new personal tidbits such as a favorite restaurant. When you're scheduled to meet with that person again, refer to your notes and suggest going to that restaurant.

3. Schedule the next meeting in your calendar at the conclusion of the meeting. Invest the time that corresponds with the importance of the relationship: a phone call, coffee or lunch accordingly.

4. Make LinkedIn a part of your Microsoft network bar to keep your contact information current. This social networking application notifies you when a contact gets a new job or promotion. Send that person a note of congratulations (the personal touch).

5. Send people a great new book, recent article, or photo that you think they will love.

These are a few tips that have enhanced my ability to network. I would love to hear some of yours. (See how I networked there? This cowgirl's got style.)

Networking skills must be developed over time, like cowgirls must work to get good at their ropin'. You must invest the time and energy to become good at anything. The benefits are immeasurable.

Purposeful networking will lead to greater business success, amazing relationships, and an ever-increasing fascination with people. Get out there and work at your ropin', Cowgirl!

CHAPTER NINE

YOU CAN LEAD A HORSE TO WATER: LEADERSHIP 101

Wendy's Words

Leadership is less about who you are

and more about who your people need you to be.

If your actions create a legacy that inspires others to dream more,

learn more, do more and become more,

then you are an excellent leader.

Dolly Parton

The wild bronco feels the weight of the cowgirl on his back as he strains against the gate to get free. The eight seconds the cowgirl must stay in the saddle is a test of wills for both horse and rider.

A bronco exudes energy. Can you imagine if the horse waltzed out of the gated corral and gingerly pranced around the stadium?

Energy is the secret ingredient to being a great leader. I define energy as the ability to get people worked up for a common cause. While some people call this charisma, I prefer the word energy. People who light up the stage have charisma. A charismatic leader is an energy magnet. She makes us want to engage. He propels us into action.

Is energy an acquired skill or one you're born with? Different perspectives abound. Anyone can become better at portraying energy.

I have a friend Annette who is an introvert. Although she was shy when I first met her, she's a ball of fire now. Did she change? No, she became comfortable enough with me over time to show me her true self. Any personality type can benefit from learning how to harness his or her own brand of energy to become a more impactful leader.

LAUGH YOUR WAY TO THE TOP

My father-in-law took my outgoing five-year-old daughter to Purple Park, our local playground. One of our neighbors saw them and shared with us how my daughter had immediately moved into supervisor mode, gathering all the playground participants into a game of pretend house. The neighbor described Madi as a *natural born leader*. Madi was five, mind you.

Whether a leader is born or made, with the role comes power, which can be used for good or evil. People don't set out to be evil dictators, but one small decision can lead to a series of actions that blur right and wrong. Your personal values ground you as a leader.

How can you stay grounded as a leader? The best way is with open and consistent feedback from those at all levels of your organization. Create a culture of open communication. Choose to be vulnerable. Ask people at the close of a staff meeting for their perceptions. Approach feedback as a gift. It is easier for people to stay silent than risk speaking the truth. It takes courage to speak up. Thank them.

Humor, I believe, is an important communication skill for a leader. Especially during stressful projects, I have found there's good reason for injecting a little humor. This grounds everyone to the fact that, while the work is important, we are not performing brain surgery. No one lives or dies as a result of their successes or failures in most jobs. By encouraging and even joining in on the fun and being able to find humor during stressful situations, a leader lightens the moment and adds an element of camaraderie in the situation.

Having a reputation of not taking myself too seriously has added some versatility to my image.

THE FEEDBACK TOOL IN YOUR TOOL BELT

My first upward feedback session was traumatic. Actually the trauma came from my anticipation of what others might say as opposed to the actual results. My dad always said that out of twenty troubles rolling toward you on a road, nineteen of them would roll into the ditch.

Think of all that wasted energy worrying about nineteen troubles that never happen.

The feedback provided me with exceptional insight into how I was perceived. My voice and tone get higher and louder when I care about a subject. I found out that my passion about a topic could be interpreted as anger. I still use this feedback daily to be more aware of my volume to ensure my intent comes across and is not derailed by others worrying about me being upset. Soliciting feedback on a regular basis provides opportunities for growth.

GO BIG OR GO HOME

Amazing leaders color outside the box. They find a better way when there doesn't seem to be one. Or rather they work with a group of people to find different ways. They ask what's the craziest, most outrageous thing we could do in this situation? This brainstorming leads to innovation and change.

Leadership is exploring, taking risks. It's like when the bull is released from the chute and your eight seconds begin. A colleague answered a question with, "Everything in me says no right now, so my answer is yes." Wow. That was courageous, and I thought differently about her.

Cowgirls who excel as leaders approach situations with an attitude of what's the greatest thing that could happen in this situation, always with a healthy respect for identifying stumbling blocks. You can't break the horse without getting in the saddle.

SIZE MATTERS WHEN IT COMES TO POSITIONAL POWER

People listen more closely to your words as you climb the corporate ladder. You have positional power. The day after I was promoted to first-level manager, I was no different from the lead technical person I had been the day before. Yet people looked at me differently. I was now supposed to be *a leader*: more knowledgeable, competent to help them in their career journey, and able to leap tall buildings.

I gave an offhanded comment to a couple of my team members that our group needed to gain more knowledge on VoIP. That afternoon, the rumor mill had me downsizing our group to bring in industry engineers with VoIP expertise. Your words have more weight when you are a leader. Own this consequence.

Chief Deputy Darlena Williams-Burnett, of the Cook County Record of Deeds Office, didn't own the weight of her words as noted in a *Chicago Tribune* article on November 29, 2007. "I manage a bunch of knuckleheads on a daily basis" (*Chicago Tribune* 2007).

Williams-Burnett was referring to one of her direct reports who hung a Christmas stocking with fake one-dollar bills peeking out near the cash register area. The decoration implied tips were being sought, a violation of county policy. How you approach an inappropriate employee must reflect professionalism and your values. Ask, listen, and then choose your words carefully.

The guy with the most positional power in the world is probably the president of the United States. We're seeing our first real women presidential candidates with Carly Fiorina and Hillary Clinton. Would a female president wield as much power as a male president?

"The American public is ready for a female president," according to Bob Beckel. "Forty years ago, about 40 percent of Americans said they wouldn't vote for a woman, even if she was qualified. Today that's down to just 10 percent– the lingering Neanderthal vote" (Beckel 2007).

Gender should not be a factor in leadership, but unfortunately we don't live in a gender-balanced world yet, either politically or professionally.

THAT PESKY GENDER MEASURING STICK

Wall Street Journal columnist Peggy Noonan contrasted former British Prime Minister Margaret Thatcher with Hillary Clinton. On the subject of toughness and how people regard it differently even in women, Noonan (2007) wrote, "Mrs. Clinton is certainly tough, to the point of hard. But toughness should have a purpose. In Mrs. Thatcher's case, its purpose was to push through a program she thought would make life better in her country. Mrs. Clinton's toughness seems to have no purpose beyond the personal accrual of power."

Noonan is using a nasty gender measuring stick to judge Hillary's behavior. Women who are strong and tough should be celebrated. The average voter thinks a president must be tough but also believes that power can—and often does—corrupt those who want it as an end and not a means. The same could be said of the average businessperson. Power is effective when it is used for right. It's not the title that makes a leader but what the leader does with that title. You can lead a horse to water, but you can't make him drink.

When women think of power as dominance, they normally hate it. When they think about power as the ability to do things, they love it because women love getting things done. An article, "Are We Our Own Worst Enemy," in the edgy magazine *Divapreneurs* builds on this issue of women and power: "Many women still choose to shelve their power or delegate it to someone else" (Delaney 2007).

Why don't we want to be responsible for our ability to effect change through the things we say publicly? The author was writing in response to a woman interviewed on *The Today Show,* who was asked, would you vote for Hillary Clinton? The woman responded that she wasn't sure because Hillary seemed so cold. It wasn't the indecision that was troubling, it was her "Hillary seems so cold" statement.

There are so many other reasons she could have given, like Hilary seems wishy-washy on the issues, or Hillary isn't up on foreign policy. She had the power to remove the strong woman stigma from her response but instead left millions of viewers reminded of how strong women are perceived as "cold and bitchy."

The use of power can be something as simple as refraining from making arbitrary and capricious comments, remarks, and judgments about our cowgirl sisters that only serve to keep perceptions alive. Give each other the support our individual power affords us. Collectively, women can change the perception of how we lead.

ONE TOUGH COOKIE

Women leaders are penalized for being tough. This could be a big reason only 4.4 percent of the CEOs of Fortune 500 companies are women as reported by Catalyst in 2015.

Good leaders are like parents; they have to know when to be tough and when to use compassion as the better tool of choice. It may not be the time to be tough when your son has wrecked the new family car. The tough love comes later as you read the situation on how he is responding to his mistake. If he takes the accident too lightly ("Well, our family has good insurance, so we'll get a new car out of this."), then the heavy hand may be necessary.

Likewise, saying there is one key to being a good leader is a pile of bull. It's like saying the broncobuster rides every horse the same way. The great cowgirl utilizes all her resources, skills, and experiences to decide the most successful way to ride her horse. A leader must look at each individual in her organization and discover what he/she needs to be most successful. It takes work, intuition, and flexibility to be a great leader. There isn't one right way to ride the bronco.

A great leader requires a toolbox of skills. To be a great woman leader you must be smarter, better prepared, and more strategic than your peers. There is no one secret to being an effective leader. Avoid the arrogance that power brings. If you want to judge someone's character, throw in a little power, and see how behavior changes. Leverage the female strength of collaboration to get feedback to ground your leadership.

As you climb the corporate ladder, people put more stock in your words. Women are the key to developing a positive perception of women leaders. Leaders must know when to be compassionate and when to be tough. As the all-around rodeo champion must master the full set of events, a great leader is required to bring her competence A-game, have awareness of her positional power, and solicit and be open to feedback, all the while remaining grounded.

CHAPTER TEN

THE COWGIRL POSSE: WOMEN SUPPORTING WOMEN

Wendy's Words

Cowgirls are only as successful as their posse.

One woman can make a difference,
but together we can rock the world.
Theglasshouseretreat.com

Growing up in Virginia, we spent Sundays at my grandparents' home. The best memories are of all us women in the warm, cozy kitchen making lunch. I have yet to find fried chicken in a restaurant (when I dare to stray from my clean eating diet) that matches Grandma's. She was the sheriff in her kitchen. My mom was her trusted deputy, and my sister and I were the posse. It was a well-oiled machine because we knew where we fit in the familial organizational structure.

My grandma was my role model for a strong, capable woman. With only a high school education, she sold Avon for over seventy-five years. She prominently displayed the large cabinet of sales awards in the epicenter living room of her four-room home. I dreamed of being that awe-inspiring sheriff full of cowgirl gumption in my own kitchen one day.

At the time, I didn't think much about the importance of having a strong posse of cowgirls who have your back yet call you on your crap. After pushing to gain credibility as the lone cowgirl in the male-dominated tech industry, I finally get the true value of such a community. A kick-ass cowgirl cultivates that posse in her climb to rodeo fame since it's a lonely trail without them.

THE LONE DARK MUSTANG

As a cowgirl's star rises, it easy to feel like that lone, dark mustang in the herd of palominos. Women deal with this isolation in different ways. It's easier in the beginning of the journey to ignore how different you are.

Jean Becker, managing director of Accenture and former engineering executive, admits, "For a while, I ignored being a woman. I didn't belong to any women's organizations. I just did my job. If anything, it was an asset to be the only woman since I stuck out. At least they wouldn't forget I was there." Jean recognized that, although her approach to the isolation worked for her, it might not for a large number of other women. Having institutional programs available for women to find their voice is imperative for companies to build a culture of inclusion for these lone white mustangs.

Silvia Travesani, co-founder of BeVisible Powered by Latina Millennials, worked with all men in the software side of the business for so many years that she actually felt more comfortable. It wasn't easy to work with the women as she moved into other parts of the business with more gender diversity.

Silvia compared the feeling of isolation in the male-dominated business world to that of being an immigrant. "Now that I've been away from Argentina for twenty years, I don't feel 100 percent there, but I don't feel 100 percent here either," she confides.

Many professional women feel this pull to fit into the boys' club while maintaining what makes us women. A cowgirl's success depends on finding her own unique way to make her place as part of the all-male trail ride while preserving her own brand of femininity.

THERE'S MILES ON THEM OLD TIRES

When asked her opinion of women in the workplace, Angela Tucci bluntly says, "There are not enough of them. I've never felt isolated, but only because I didn't come to my professional life with that mental model. I came to work as a person, not as a woman. I feel strongly that we each should be treated as a person. But I learned that this may not be common across my gender."

Angela recognized that not all women come into the workplace treating their gender as an afterthought. With more mileage, the toll of isolation gets heavier, making the community of a posse more important to the success of even the strongest cowgirl.

Madeleine Albright is the poster child of the strong, capable woman. She pulled no punches with her quote about women working together, "There's a special place in hell for women who don't help other women."

I am amazed at how few quotes exist on the professional woman-to-woman relationships. Even more interesting is how few of those quotes are positive ones. One woman, Mariela Dabbah, even started the "Red Shoe Movement," challenging her audience to create women-supporting-women quotes. Now that's Cowgirling Up!

HERE'S A LOT TO LOVE ABOUT THOSE COWGIRLS

Cheryl Campbell, senior vice president of Excel Energy, says she likes the relationship aspect of how women interact. Cheryl says, "Women are more willing to build relationships. It makes me crazy how men will have a disagreement, say f*&# you, and then go off and have a beer. The issue they were fighting about hasn't been resolved. It still needs to be talked through."

Women are willing to have the conversation to put the issue to bed in support of the relationship. The easiest way to do this is to ask, "Are we really on the same page?" to ensure we get to a better place after the conflict."

Mary Baum, president BA&T, describes women working with women as "not having as many barriers when working together. If there is a barrier, a woman is willing to talk about it. With men, you have to figure it out." The female approach of being in service to the relationship is especially important in business since a company's success is routinely linked to the strength of their customer relationships.

Maggie Wilderotter, executive chair of Fortune 500 company Frontier Communications, supports the strength of these relational skills that women bring to the table with her quote in CNN online, "Women are very good at multitasking, have a sixth sense with people, are nurturing and service-oriented."

I've heard women describe what it's like working with other women as being able to talk in short hand, not even having to finish the sentence. This is especially true when talking through complex issues. Jean Becker shares how hard she had to work to explain in a way that men could hear and understand.

THE POTTY IS A LONELY PLACE

One woman I interviewed confided she sometimes missed having someone to go to the restroom with on breaks. Having a bathroom buddy didn't make the ten top list of what my forty-five female executive interviewees love about working with women though. The collaboration, the empathy, and the desire to build great relationships did.

These positives contribute to the limiting expectations that all female bosses must be softer and gentler in their leadership style. This is its own form of unconscious bias, and I've also been guilty of judging women for not having an open and approachable demeanor.

I met Carly Fiorina earlier in my career at one of our corporate events, and although impressed with her positional power, I was disappointed she lacked approachability and warmth. What worried me the most was her success as a high-profile female executive in the spotlight reinforced the stereotype that to be successful, women have to act like men. Those darn saddlebags (baggage) were leaking out again.

WHEN COWGIRLS FIGHT

When asking my female interviewees what they liked most and least about working with women, I was surprised the majority started with three negative stereotypes: women are catty, hold grudges, and hate to cry at work.

My two best friends and I went on a girl's trip every January to get a little sliver of sun and beach in those cold Colorado winters. It was a cowgirl party, a totally indulgent self-fest. Our only decision-making responsibilities were which books to read for pleasure and which fruity drinks to order next.

Our numbers crept up each year as word spread. Things were going well until the year we ventured to Aruba with eight diverse women. What a surprise when we noticed the cliques forming and the little squabble between women.

Damn, how did we turn into those women? Being the middle child, nurtured as a mediator of our tribe of three close knit kids, I prided myself on getting along with most anyone. But I couldn't wait to vote these bitches off the island. Enough with high maintenance women! I was done.

Our original posse spent the next couple of trips dissecting what went wrong, like the Southern woman trying to find that tipping point of the exact right level of syrupy sugar in her famous sweet tea. We realized the secret to the right women depended on the emotional intelligence (EQ) of each woman on the trip. Think of EQ as being smart about your feelings. *Psychology Today* defines it as the ability to identify and manage your own emotions and the emotions of others. It describes EQ as three main skills:

1. Emotional awareness, including the ability to identify your own emotions and those of others;
2. Ability to harness emotions and apply them to tasks like thinking and problem solving;
3. Ability to manage and regulate your own emotions, and the ability to cheer up or calm down another person.

Emotional intelligence will be one of the top ten most important job skills in 2020, according to the 2016 World Economic Forum's Future of Jobs Report as reported by Harvey Deutschendorf.

It's not the percentage of cowgirls that determines the level of dysfunction in a team. A group of emotionally intelligent women create a kick-ass business team, and could enjoy a fabulous no-drama girls' trip. No one ever asks how many men are too many in a group.

When asked, when will there be enough women on the Supreme Court, Justice Ruth Bader Ginsburg quipped, "When there are nine."

She went on to share, "People are shocked with my answer. But there have been nine men, and nobody's ever raised a question about that."

Men and women describe women working together as "it could get catty." I once went eight full weeks without another woman in a conference call or meeting while an SVP at a software company. It was pretty hard to be catty when I wasn't interacting with another woman.

There is a concept in social psychology called "in-group favoritism" where people favor members of their own social group (Brewer, 1979, 2007). One might assume based on the research that women are treated more positively by other women, and women evaluate women higher in performance reviews. Yet most of us have experiences that refute this. Women hold grudges against other women for years, whereas men have a knock-down, drop-dead fight, then shake it off as they walk out of the conference room.

Cheryl Campbell shares her experience, "Women tend to be harder on each other. I have no patience with women not being upfront and transparent with each other. Women act this way more than men. As women grow in their careers, I see a lot less women holding grudges. They are more upfront, maybe mimicking more male characteristics."

When asked if women ran an industry, what norms would change, Robin Szeliga shares, "I'm curious if it would be a more forgiving corporate environment. I want to think it would but I'm not sure since women tend to hold on to their emotions longer. It's our thoughts that spark our emotions, which in turn drive behavior. If a self-aware woman were to run an industry, might it look different than how a self-aware man would run it? I would speculate that it's more about self-awareness than gender."

As self-aware women and men, we choose everyday whether to reaffirm these big three stereotypes of women being catty, competitive and holding grudges. We must first recognize the bias in our attitude to create change. A cowgirl can't stop something she can't see.

THE DOUBLE-EDGED SWORD

Empathy makes us better leaders. Crying at work supports the stereotype that women are too emotional and weak. Yet this same physiological makeup that makes it easier for us to cry actually serves us by enabling us to put ourselves in someone else's shoes and empathize with their fear, pain, or joy.

Jean Becker, managing director at Accenture, shared her experiences with managing emotions in the workplace, "Toward the end of my time at McData, I cried twice with my boss when frustrated with a situation. I was so pissed at myself. I realized I could only identify frustration and anger when it was happening. I didn't have the awareness to recognize the precursor emotions leading up to shedding the tears."

Becker now mentors women to look at the situation in hindsight and break down why they were angry or frustrated, getting clear of the steps and feelings leading up to the anger or frustration.

Identifying the early warning signs allows one to recognize and deal with the emotion earlier. When you feel those precursor emotions like that tightness in the gut, or start to feel teary, you'll get better at backing off it by asking, "could we talk about this facet of it instead," which is not a trigger. Getting better at managing your emotions will allow you to embrace your soft side in the workplace. The crowd loves the authentic cowgirl who is not afraid of showing emotion when she wins the rodeo.

THE ESTROGEN STANDOFF

Does the lone cowgirl in the roping event like the notoriety that comes from being the only one? Jean shared that it helped her stand out being the only woman in the executive suite. She comments, "If anything, it was an asset since it was harder to forget I was in the room."

I loved being the only girl in the Shoot, Dribble and Pass contest at my high school. It pushed me to work harder. It even made getting second place more rewarding, especially since I beat my twin brother. I wore my competitive nature like a badge of honor, cross-stitching and framing my mantra, "Anything boys can do, girls can do better."

Being competitive doesn't have to be a negative, so why do some women approach the women under them not as comrades-in-arms but as threats to be countered?

One theory suggests women may not support each other's progress in situations where men outnumber them. The research found that female supervisors were less supportive of female employees in male-dominated organizations (Ryan et al. 2012).

Would a cowgirl actually pull up the ladder after breaking the glass ceiling?

WHY WOMEN ARE COMPETITIVE: THE NEUROSCIENCE

David Rock, of the NeuroLeadership Institute, found that when people realize they are being compared with others, a threat response in their brains sends cortisol levels skyrocketing and makes it hard for them to take in other information. When a threat response is activated, the brain allocates fewer resources to the prefrontal cortex making us a little "dumber" for a while. These resources are needed to activate and sustain other areas of the brain where automated fight-or-flight reactions are managed.

I can attribute some portion of women not supporting women's behavior to Rock's threat response theory. But we women have a lot going on simultaneously in our lives. In my experience, my own bags are responsible for a large part of my responses to situations.

The way women feel about other women is a reflection of how we feel about ourselves. Our own insecurities make us afraid to share knowledge, support, and power. These insecurities drive intense emotions, which drive the catty competitive behavior.

One executive I interviewed said, "A female executive fairly high up in the organization was a long shot for a job. She wasn't outright hostile or anti-women, but she had big elbows—not letting other women around her. I don't remember her being that way before."

This executive recalled the leader as shaky in her new role, concluding that those insecurities might be related to her *big elbows attitude*. Confidence is closely linked to a cowgirl's success in the corporate arena.

THE TOKEN FEMALE EXECUTIVE

The executive team may feel one woman is enough to satisfy the activists' pressure and have company representation at "diversity" venues.

Take a look at the executive team landscape, and you'll see there's only one lone spot for a female. This open seat is treated like a part of the male executive team's strategic to-do list: let's find one female to add to the team to check our diversity box.

The 2015 research by Cristian Dezső, an associate professor at University of Maryland's Robert H. Smith School of Business, and two co-authors, David Gaddis Ross and Jose Uribe of Columbia Business School, found evidence of a "quota" effect.

Smith Brain Trust summarized Dezső's research in their article on March 25, 2015, as "Once a company had appointed one woman to a top-tier job, the chances of a second woman landing an elite position at the same firm dropped by about 50 percent."

"They try pretty hard to get a woman on their top management team, but then they will stop," said Ross, a co-author of the study. "What I think our paper shows is that it's going to be harder for the low number of women in top management to be a problem that solves itself."

Ross suggests, "If women are competitively vying for top positions, it's not arising from some kind of innate female quality, but from the behavior of the men and their colleagues."

Status is defined as our social need for comparative importance, significance, and a place in the social pecking order. Studies have found that for our brains, social status—how we are viewed in our work environment—is more rewarding and important than money. In the workplace, a threat to status is being left out of the group.

According to 2015 Catalyst research, women make up percent of the total workforce in the S&P 500 companies. Of these, 36.8 percent are midlevel managers, 25.1 percent are senior executives, 19.2 percent are board members, and only 4 percent are CEOs.

The percentages decline at each higher level in the organization. So it's natural to feel the threat response at each subsequent level of the corporate ladder when there are statistically fewer and fewer women.

Moving more women into leadership positions is a complex problem. Ownership of the problem has to be shared by women and men. As David Rock suggests, neurologically, women naturally feel pitted against one another due to the lone spot available to them as well as against executive men protecting the status quo.

STUNG BY THE QUEEN BEE

Some women move past this threat response and give a hand up to women below them while others don't. *Queen Bee* is the term coined for a woman who can't move past it. This female boss has zero interest in fostering the careers of women who aim to follow in her footsteps, and she may attempt to cut them off at the pass.

The term *Queen Bee Syndrome* was coined in 1974, following a study by researchers at the University of Michigan. They examined promotion rates and the impact of the women's movement on the workplace in a survey of more than twenty thousand reader responses in *Psychology Today* and *Redbook*.

The research found that women who achieved success in male-dominated environments were at times likely to oppose the rise of other women. This occurred, they argued, largely because the patriarchal culture of work encouraged the few women who rose to the top to become obsessed with maintaining their authority.

While leading the presentation of a new project proposal recently, and remember this is four decades after this survey, I came head to head with the biggest Queen Bee I have ever met in my thirty-year professional career. Over the course of one hour, this Queen Bee offered zero positive comments on the work of the group, sharing only negative feedback. Reminding everyone in the room of her trail boss status, she concluded the meeting with, "I am who I am and won't change for you or anyone." A cowgirl must know what she'll do before she runs into that Queen Bee.

EITHER WE'RE PART OF THE PROBLEM, OR WE'RE PART OF THE SOLUTION

A high performer never brings a problem without having a solution in her back pocket. It's our job to call out bad behavior, but we must hate the game, not the player. It takes courage to confront a woman who is not supporting other women and find a way to not simply maintain but leave the relationship stronger.

Mary Baum worked with the head of professional services within a company. Unfortunately, there was ambiguity in each of their responsibilities, and the woman acted like a child, responding defensively to attempts to work together and talking behind Mary's back. Mary endured the behavior for months hoping her peer would recognize what Mary had to offer.

Finally Mary reached out to her and asked, "Can you tell me what I'm doing that undermines our relationship?"

The other woman responded that she heard Mary had said this and that. Mary refuted the rumors and asked if they could start over and build a more honest relationship. As their relationship improved, so did the work issues. One day the other woman confided that she'd always had to protect her turf at the company and had assumed the same when Mary came on board.

A cowgirl must courageously let down her guard to seek first to understand a Queen Cowgirl's perspective. Our willingness to be open is sometimes all it takes to reset that clean slate.

It will take every professional woman to make Queen Bees a thing of the past. Michael Frendo, SVP of engineering at Polycom, suggests women show their support for other women by mentoring them and sharing advice about what has made them successful.

We must create a sense of we're all in this together. Michael admitted he doesn't see enough mentoring from women. He suggests women not only practice this in their professional environments, but also volunteer in middle schools as role models to the next set of leaders. Michael adds, "There is definitely less impact [on female students] if a man goes back to middle schools as a role model." Both middle school girls and boys need to see examples of strong professional women to become their norm.

YOU CAN'T BE IT IF YOU CAN'T SEE IT

Incredible female role models can inspire us to push higher in our professional journey. They let us see what we can be.

I'll never forget settling into the hospital bed after delivering my first child. I couldn't imagine feeling or looking as good as the perky, smiling, one-day-old new mom in the opposite bed. But because I saw it, I could be it... by tomorrow, of course.

Unfortunately, most of the women I interviewed had few, if any, females between them and the CEO, so they succeeded in spite of not being able to see it. Trailblazing women owe it to the ones behind them to mark the path.

Angela Tucci, Rally Software acquired by CA Technologies executive, shares, "I think we have enough women coming into the corporate environment, but we're losing them because they are exiting too early or they choose a different path because there aren't role models ahead of them. A sales woman sees all the middle-age white males high-fiving each other in her organization, and thinks, *If this is what success looks like, that is not for me.* There's not enough modeling of executive women to give us an example of what we could become."

The very presence of women in positions of power can serve as a subconscious confidence boost and result in women taking more risks. Witnessing other female leaders can help women break down their own stereotypes in regards to their own gender.

The National Center for Women and Information Technology (NCWIT) has a "Sit with Me" campaign, aimed at slowing the exodus of midlevel women in corporate America. The program creates videos of women sitting in a red chair, telling their stories about being in a male-dominated field. The idea is by telling our stories we unite and feel less alone. When we feel alone is when we opt out.

I've created a video podcast series, *Gamechangers,* to share the inspirational stories of successful professional women and men who are authentically creating gender-intelligent cultures within the business community. Check out the series on my website, www.corporatecowgirlup.com. How will you Cowgirl Up to make extinct the damaging stereotype that women don't support other women?

THE VALUE OF MENTORS AND SPONSORS

Mentors are an important way for women to feel less alone. Having role models to approach for advice and guidance is imperative to your success. But being considered for bigger roles is where a sponsor comes into play.

By the time high-profile jobs make it to being posted, a list of candidates has already been created through internal politics.

Roxanne Varza, director at Halle Freyssinet, succinctly describes the difference of having a mentor and a sponsor. "A mentor is coaching you whereas a sponsor is speaking on your behalf."

We have a culture in the business world of providing mentoring programs for women, but I've never seen a corporate sponsorship program for women because sponsoring is done beneath the radar. No one sponsors you unless they have a relationship with you and know the caliber of your personality and your work. Sponsorship means fighting for someone to get an opportunity.

When asked how mentoring or sponsorship has helped Angela Tucci in her career, she responded, "There is a big distinction between mentoring and sponsoring. Sponsors take action. Women need to do more sponsoring of other high-performing women. Don't just coach me, open doors for me. Take action. Expecting managers and leaders in the organization to take action to make the women they sponsor better and provide opportunities or challenges to help them progress is a common expectation."

When men mentor men, they provide guidance and knowledge about the operation and driving financial performance of the business. When men mentor women, their support comes in the form of helping women with negotiation and the softer skills, such as how to present with confidence, and how to own a room.

Women are steered into support or administrative executive positions, like HR and IT. These support positions don't provide the business acumen skill set required of most General Manager or C-level positions.

Margaret McLean, general counsel and chief risk officer of TeleTech, says, "Companies should require their leaders to mentor up-and-coming women and make sure they are offered Profit and Loss (P&L) positions even if it means taking smaller roles with P&L responsibility. You need to have your own ship you're piloting. Make sure up-and-coming women are not left behind."

When asked if they would ever sponsor a woman just because she was a woman, the male and female executives I spoke with responded with a resounding no!

I agree with those executives. Making a decision to sponsor a woman over a better-qualified candidate would be inconsistent with my integrity and challenge the relationships I have built.

WE CAN'T BE IT IF THEY DON'T SEE US

Women will only advance into higher levels of leadership if they can get their names in the hat for those big positions. A cowgirl must cultivate sponsorship in the movers and shakers—those executives who have a say in the shell game as openings come up and changes are made across the organization.

Sponsors look for candidates who are serious about succeeding. We must show up prepared and competent. We must exude the confidence and executive presence that we can handle anything that comes our way. A sponsor risks their political capital to go to bat for us only if there is a consistency of performance and a relationship warranting their trust. We must build a reputation for delivering and exhibiting versatility in the face of change and crisis.

WAYS TO CULTIVATE SPONSORSHIP

- Do great work.
- Don't wait to be noticed for your successes. Men don't.
- Promote successes so others know we rocked it.
- Know our worth, and be confident about what we bring to the table.
- Ask those who could be your sponsors what is needed to be considered for bigger roles.

THERE IS A SPECIAL PLACE IN HEAVEN FOR MEN AND WOMEN WHO SPONSOR WOMEN

To move the dial toward more women in leadership requires a new level of intention and commitment to mentor and sponsor them. Men sponsor men because they are men. Women sponsor women in spite of them being women. Let's change this perception. Our new motto will be: *There is a special place in heaven for men and women who sponsor women.*

LET'S BRING IT HOME, SISTA

Working with all men takes its toll on a cowgirl over time. Build your posse to gain the support needed to manage the isolation. Then bask in the empathetic, nurturing, and intuitive relationships you have with these other women. Seek first to understand the Queen Bees whose behavior is more tied to their own stuff than yours.

Celebrate those female and male leaders who are creating a gender-intelligent business world, voicing appreciation for their way of showing up in the world. Let their example motivate you to Cowgirl Up to mentor and sponsor those behind you, repaying the help each of you got on your corporate ride to the top. Cowgirls are only as successful as their posses!

CHAPTER ELEVEN

BEANS AND FRANKS WITHOUT THE BEANS ARE JUST HOTDOGS: THE POWER OF WOMEN AND MEN IN BUSINESS

Wendy's Words

It's not about fixing women to be more like men.

And it's definitely not about blaming men

for the lack of women in leadership.

It's about finding the 1+1=3 of men and women working together to

collaboratively create and exponentially expand outcomes.

You don't have to be anti-man to be pro-woman.

Jane Galvin Lewis

Visiting the rodeo for the first time is like attending your first women's conference. It's a whole new world to see so many people who look like you and have the same passion for self-improvement.

Women's conferences give us the chance to experience a rare environment of camaraderie with other female professionals taking a break from the mostly male, high-paced, results-driven business climate to meet professional women and hear inspirational speakers share their journey and wisdom.

At my first company women's conference, I vividly remember the story told by the keynote speaker and the tone of his voice as he told it.

As family tradition, his kids took turns cutting the homemade French apple pie made so lovingly by Mom every Thanksgiving. It was his daughter's turn that year to carefully cut into the warm pie. As the cinnamon smell drifted upward from that first slice, the young girl proudly presented the piece to him as the head of the house.

I watched the speaker's rugged face soften and heard his voice grow quiet as he recalled his daughter's demeanor moving from delight at being the chosen one for a brief moment, to slowly and more soberly confiding her own whispered realization: "I'll never get the first piece of pie, Dad."

Visibly moved, he told the audience this was the first time he had realized professional women have inherent disadvantages simply by the anatomy they were born with and that he should be a part of trying to solve the problem.

I COULD JUST FIX HIM

Many women look at the men in their lives—in the workplace or in the home—as projects. You have to accept where men are. I've done a lot of *if onlys* with my "work husbands." If only he would act this way or that way. As tempting as it may be to pull out the castration tools, achieving gender equality is not about making men like women, or vice versa.

It would be easy to blame men for the lack of women in leadership, but this will not solve the problem. We've tried the blame game already. As Ben Franklin said, "The definition of insanity is doing the same things over and over again and expecting different results."

It is definitely not fair, but at 75 percent of the executive suite, men are the gatekeepers for women gaining increased entry into all levels of leadership. We have to have their help. Making change calls for a radical new approach. What's radical is working to understand the differences and being intentional about taking advantage of those differences, rather than banging our heads against the barn wall.

THOSE DARN GENES

When a woman tries on a pair of jeans in the changing room of a store and finds them too tight, she thinks she needs to eat better and find time to go to the gym. When a man tries on a pair of jeans and finds them to be too small, he wonders what the hell is wrong with the jeans. The two responses could not be more different to the same situation.

Two law students, a male and a female, are asked in their freshman year why they are having trouble with the intense law school program.

The female student answers that she is not smart enough, while the male student explains the curriculum is too hard.

Seeking first to understand the differences men and women bring to situations is required to gain gender intelligence and take advantage of the uniqueness we bring.

IT'S TIME TO PUT ON YOUR BIG GIRL RODEO PANTS

The secret to winning the rodeo lies in our ability to first know what we don't know. It's hard to fix something when we don't know what's broken. The thing that keeps tripping us up is something called unconscious bias, those deep-rooted preferences that we may be totally unaware of. You may only be aware of one or two of them, but you probably have a whole slew of those boogers.

Both women and men are saddled with unconscious bias. If you've ever judged a mom who hightails it out of the office to pick up her kid on time, you've been guilty of unconscious bias. If you've ever been surprised to find a man as the chief HR leader, you've been guilty of unconscious bias. If you've ever assumed the woman in the room was a secretary instead of the CEO, you've been guilty of unconscious bias.

We can't get rid of our unconscious biases, but we can become aware of them. We need to intentionally begin the practice of rewiring our thinking. It's by repetitive reframing that we develop those gender intelligence muscles until they become second nature. The more individuals we can get to do this, the more we'll have a collective shift. That's when we'll begin to see real momentum toward gender equality.

AREN'T WE DOING IT ALREADY?

Isn't the gender equality movement already afoot? Gender equality makes the news daily. I regularly read articles about gender equality. It's the catchphrase of the day. Everyone wants to say they are doing something, but are they really? Much of the stuff in the media is surface stuff that doesn't move the dial. It's using the catchphrases to get on a list of top one hundred places to work. Isn't that pinkwashing the topic?

Visibility will not create the action needed to bring equality of the sexes in the workplace. The problem goes much deeper than the headlines suggest, and a more innovative approach is necessary to create change. No cowgirl will ever break into the all-male trail boss club without the intentional action of the cowboy sharing the keys to the executive chow hall.

I'm not throwing potshots at the guys. The majority of men aren't inherently evil in their treatment of women in the workplace and probably are oblivious to their behavior and its impact. In fact, in the course of writing this book, I've met men who are fabulous feminist advocates, like John Kelley of Cerescan and Greg Greenstreet of Twitter Boulder. These men make gender equality their own issue.

One of my favorite equality advocates is Canadian Prime Minister Justin Trudeau who publicized his intent to fifty-fifty gender parity in the Parliament. At Trudeau's swearing-in ceremony, the prime minister responded, "Because it's 2015," when asked why he named fifteen women and fifteen men to his cabinet (Frisk, 2015).

There are not enough enlightened cowboys willing to share the executive chow hall keys. When asking the forty-five executive women interviewees for this book if they could recommend a male leader who gets it in terms of being a great advocate for women, in most cases I got a long pause following by the comment, "Let me think about that."

There is no silver bullet that will get us to fifty-fifty representation. Women can't move into more executive positions on their own. They need the help of men. Men are starting to cowboy up to get involved because they see the financial and organizational benefits.

HELP LIKE COOPER

A fabulous example of men Cowboying Up played out in Hollywood. Academy Award-winning Jennifer Lawrence penned an incisive opinion about what it was like to discover via a Sony e-mail hack that she made 7 percent as opposed to the 9 percent of gross sales made by her male costars, Christian Bale, Jeremy Renner, and Bradley Cooper, on the film, *American Hustle.*

Even though Lawrence isn't hard up for money, after initially not pursuing the disparity, she decided to negotiate for the difference because not doing so would contribute to the systemic issue of unequal pay.

In response, one of her costars, Cooper, pledged publicly to support pay equity by being transparent with his future pay negotiations for any film with female cast members. "There's a double standard in the whole world, yeah, for sure. This is just one aspect," Cooper said as quoted on ET online.

Women need to speak up for the sake of other women, like Lawrence did. Men need to speak up for women, like Cooper did.

After joining an all-male board, Su, a female executive, noticed that every time she spoke, the chairman would look at José, the man beside her, to see how he reacted to what Su was saying. The chairman wouldn't even look at Su when she was talking. Su took José aside and asked for his help. The next time the chairman looked at José, he responded to the chairman, "Su's got this. She knows exactly what's going on." The chairman never looked at José again when Su was talking. We each need the other person to take the stand in our business arena.

IT'S NOT ONLY THE BOOBIES THAT MAKE US DIFFERENT

When I tell people I have a twin, they often ask if we are identical. I respond by saying, "No, there are two main differences (pointing to my southern region and chest)."

My brother and I approach things differently, but we both agree that we're part of one family and have each other's back, an attitude we should practice in the workplace.

Yes, men and women are different. Denying those differences almost makes us regress in this race to equality. These differences account for the majority of conflicts, and dare I say inequality in the workplace. By understanding the differences, we're busting open the gates allowing us to embrace them instead of fighting them as different from our own cowgirl way.

I've been told most of my life that to understand someone different, I need to walk a mile in his or her boots. That's often easier said than done, but because it's hard doesn't mean you roll over and play dead. Research is proving the financial benefits of having gender equality and more women in the workplace, but it's not about the money. The mix created when men and women pull together is much more nuanced and has more depth. We collectively come up with more innovative products and solutions. Beans are boring by themselves, and franks without the fixings are pretty bland.

As a director of an engineering department, I once invited a male to attend the company's annual women's conference. Marty, a seemingly gender-enlightened project manager, responded to my invite with, "I would feel so uncomfortable as the only man in a ballroom full of women."

I gave him a sarcastic grin. "Wow, I wouldn't know how that feels."

Marty did attend the conference and gained valuable insight into the solitary trail women walk in the male-dominated business world. He later confided that he'd hesitated to join in on table discussions and approaching groups of women at the coffee station. "Even though it was uncomfortable being the lone male in those situations, I'm so glad I had this experience," he told me. "I never thought it would be this hard." I watched as he went on to become a softer, gentler project manager who was able to advocate for his female peers.

Walking a mile in another person's proverbial boots can be accomplished by learning how our male and female brains work differently. This knowledge helps women as much as men understand how we interact and what we expect of each other in the workplace. Increasing our gender intelligence and moving toward a complementary leadership model starts with understanding each other better. We can then leverage each other's strengths to help us collectively succeed.

WE'RE BOTH SMARTY PANTS

Gender in our brains is chromosomally and neurologically locked-in much like our personality or eye color.

PET scans, MRIs, and SPECT imaging allow scientists to get an incredibly clear picture of which parts of the brain light up when we do certain things. Research has found that men and women are equally smart, but each sex uses different parts of the brain to solve problems or achieve goals.

As we explore this brain difference information, it's important to emphasize that most of the statements are not absolutes. For example, *typically* men's brains go into a rest state more often than women's do, and *typically* women have larger areas in the brain dedicated to tracking gut feeling.

Yet some individuals are closer on the gender spectrum for the opposite gender than others. Examples might be the man who's always been more verbal than most men, or a tech woman who exhibits more male brain attributes. While there are always exceptions, understanding the research-based gender differences will help men and women better understand each other in the workplace.

IF ONLY WE WERE ALL ALIKE

The differences in our brains account for much of the conflict males and females find in working together in business. For instance, the emotional processing through our midbrain (limbic system) is dramatically different for a man or a woman.

A woman can process a major emotion-laden experience immediately, whereas a man may take hours to do so. Suppose a woman wants to talk about a tragedy immediately after it occurs, but a man clearly needs some time to process the event. His silence may be read as being cold or unfeeling. Awareness of these differences in emotional processing can prevent or diffuse tension between men and women in the home and in the workplace.

I will caution you to use this male-female brain difference for good and never evil. For instance, knowing that female retinas have more P ganglion cells— which see color and fine detail— while male retinas have more M ganglion cells, which more easily see physical motion of objects, could be used as your defense when you didn't see the approaching car at the intersection as quickly as he did. In these cases, to preserve harmony, the most effective approach is to say, "Thanks for watching out for us, honey," to your loving spouse as he points out the quickly approaching car in a highly engaged tone of voice.

Brain differences account for differences in how and what we remember, how we experience the world, what we buy and why we buy it, and even how we process words. For instance, women use more words than men while speaking, reading, and writing. Men can find this helpful when they realize that they process less through their brain's cingulate gyrus (the part of the brain that runs life experiences around in your head), which makes them focus more on the facts. Do you see more men working without talking than women? Do you see fewer men than women in your workplace thinking out problems in words related to feelings? Understanding neurological differences in how we communicate can lead to increased gender intelligence and better leveraging of each other.

THERE'S NO CRYING IN THE RODEO

My experience and interviews found women cry most often at work when they are frustrated or angry. Crying is a biological reaction to stress, an emotional reset valve that is more easily triggered in women than in men. I've heard in my own career, "Don't ever let them see you cry." But it's not unprofessional to bring your emotions to work, it's human. You can't make an important presentation or decide what to wear to work without emotions being involved.

There are physical reasons why women cry quicker than men. The higher testosterone levels in men make it harder to cry. Women have higher levels of prolactin, which controls the development of tear glands (Gurian and Annis, 2008,14). Tear glands and prolactin are what produce tears, so women produce more tears. Men have larger tear ducts whereas women have narrower tear ducts. If a man and woman both tear up, the woman's tears will spill onto her cheeks quicker (Dahl 2015). Also, women have far more cells in the part of the brain that controls empathy, so they are more sensitive to emotional situations.

Men cry at work in sentimental situations as opposed to during stress or frustration. Sir Winston Churchill was known as a crier, tearing up routinely throughout the Second World War most often as an emotional response to kind words of appreciation.

Men report feeling better after crying at work, whereas women feel worse. A gender-intelligent cowboy sees himself as a powerful but emotional being. He understands the power and value of having others see him share his emotions in the workplace.

WHAT'S A COWBOY TO DO?

Many male managers are uncomfortable with displays of emotion at work, especially tears. So what's a male manager to do when a woman cries?

First, he might take a breath and remember that biologically, she's more prone to tears. He might then tell her it's okay to share her feelings, that it actually shows how much she cares about the situation. Then he might offer her a bandana (I mean tissue) from his denim shirt pocket. Such a response shows more gender intelligence in a difficult situation.

A gender-intelligent workplace better leverages the strengths of each individual, even a woman's physiological tendency to cry. The male positive aggression can move us forward at times in leadership, but female capabilities, such as empathy and rapport building, are equally important. The balance can be powerful and will improve the collective outcome.

A mixed-gender team uses the male and female assets to achieve more than they could individually.

THE MASCULINE-FEMININE ENERGY DANCE

Women aren't all feminine energy, and men aren't all masculine energy. A large number of strong female executives I've met, worked with, and interviewed for this book consistently embody strong masculine energy. I suspect this energy was nurtured by being in the male-dominated business arena. Likewise, Annie Oakley's cut-and-dried demeanor was most definitely nurtured from working side by side with cowboys during her career. The ability to leverage mixed-gender teams is impacted by the masculine and feminine energy we each possess.

A feminine tendency is to value and adhere to process in getting the work of the organization done. There is an advantage to following a repeatable process for a solution, service, or product.

Conversely, action is an example of a masculine tendency. Action is making a decision to move forward. I've been in start-ups with all action and no process. Without repeatable process, each product development release was a slugfest to get to delivery. Yes, it seemed advantageous to get a product out quickly, but doing so often negatively impacted quality. I've also been in large corporations where we spend more time on process than on product development, not the optimal approach either.

This idea of a win-win achieved by a mix of feminine and masculine across a team is illustrated in the book, *Leadership and the Sexes* (Gurian and Annis, 2008, 39):

> *A gender-balanced team responded to a Response for Proposal (RFP). When the team went in to pitch to the potential client, they relied on two men, with similar masculine gender styles, to do most of the presentation.*

As they were leaving the room, the two men congratulated each other, sure they had won the deal. The two women on the team warned of what they had seen on the faces of the customer panel members, especially two crucial people.

The two men disagreed with the women's assessment, emphasizing they had addressed every single point asked for in the RFP. The men were replaying the agenda; the women were connecting to the faces, moods and the underlying tone of the room.

When the pitch team came together to decide if there was a need for a second presentation to the potential client, the men saw no need. No follow-up meeting was held, and unfortunately the deal was lost. The retrospective feedback from the potential client confirmed that the women had been right and it was the two panel members that had killed the deal.

As Michael Gurian and Barbara Annis so eloquently summarize in their book, "Gender-intelligent men will often trust what women 'saw' during a contract negotiation. Studies completed all over the world, over the last twenty years, confirm that women in general read signals on faces better than men do; they are also better at reading gestures and other subtleties. Women often can remember later during debriefing—more of what they saw during the negotiation, and thus interpret well the direction the negotiation may be going."

Awareness of what each gender brings creates an enlightened approach to leadership in an organization. Gender-intelligent teams can leverage these feminine strengths to improve business outcomes.

CLINT IS A MAN'S MAN

The previous lost-deal example should in no way imply that women are better at business than men. Our most important take-away is to recognize that each person has a combination of both masculine and feminine energy that serves him or her as a leader.

Dare I say that even Clint Eastwood, the epitome of the real man, has some soft edges of feminine energy. Look at his character in *Bridges of Madison County*, carefree wanderer turned hopeful romantic after a chance meeting with his soul mate.

There's a masculine/feminine polarity where having access to both sides is an asset. Going to either extreme is dangerous. Workplace cultures should embrace men who present a stronger soft side and women who portray a more masculine demeanor to allow both to be their authentic selves.

It's not about moving from the 82 percent male-dominated executive suite and boardroom to an 82 percent female-dominated one. We can only get to our best collective by having an equal representation of balanced leadership. In rodeo roping, the roper is only as good as the horse. The same is true in business.

WATCH YOUR BACK, COWGIRL!

Jennifer Joyce, a transformative relationship coach, whose majority of work has been with male-dominated corporations such as telecommunication and oil and gas, started a new assignment, working with all female peers. She soon found the group thought she was a problem. She was shocked since she loved the work and assumed things were going well. She didn't know why it was happening, even doubting herself and her abilities. At the same time, she was working with a mentor and learning about polarity management, an approach to managing unsolvable problems. Effective talent management stresses the importance of recognizing the positives and negatives of the feminine and masculine energies. Results are more robust with *both/and* rather than *either/or*. Jennifer realized the source of the conflict. The group was working strongly from the feminine point of view, which caused them to drop into negative feminine characteristics.

Jennifer found that she was bringing more masculine energy as compensation for the heavily weighted feminine energy of the group. She pushed goals, structure, and accountability in a way that disrupted their usual routines. In the group's opinion, Jennifer was the problem. Instead of talking to her directly, the women talked behind her back, a common behavior of the negative feminine.

Jennifer reconnected with her guiding principles to present her best self in the situation. Authenticity was the most important principle for her. She realized she had to be authentic with herself first before she could do it with anyone else. Jennifer also needed the courage to do what was needed in the moment. She understood that both authenticity and courage lived in the masculine polarity. In order to be balanced, she also brought the feminine attribute of compassion—for herself and for her team.

At the staff meeting the next day, the same undercurrent of negativity about her surfaced. Jennifer stopped the meeting and said, "This is the vision I hold for us. One that says there's space for what I bring to the team and also for what you each bring. We are all big enough and smart enough to hold room for both. Together we will be a stronger, more balanced team. I invite you to embrace this vision too."

The women in the room heard her and changed.

BEWARE OF THE DARK SIDE

The stronger partnerships, teams, or organizations maintain a balance between masculine and feminine polarity. If either polarity is weaker or missing, the team dynamics move to the negative of the stronger side.

Look at our current culture, particularly in business and politics. We are more heavily weighted on the masculine side. We know this world as the negative masculine, also known as the *patriarchy*. The military is a great example of a patriarchal approach.

Lisa Calkins, CEO of Amadeus, described the negative masculine in this way:

I noticed we were having a conflict with a client and the men in the room responded with "I'm right, and dammit, I'm going to make sure they know I'm right and why they're wrong."

This dig-in-our-heels approach is not how I would handle the situation. I saw it so differently. There are times when you have to stand up and beat your chest and say, "I'm right dammit and here is how it is going to be." There are also times where you don't go to war.

To overgeneralize, men are about the war and women are about the peace. There are times when collaborative negotiators get to a better outcome. There are times when standing up for yourself and being warlike is necessary. To me the reason our company is so successful is because of its respect for both.

IT'S *AND,* NOT *OR*

One downside of the negative masculine is a corporate culture of profits at the expense of process and people. By bringing in the feminine, it can be *and* instead of *or*.

Angela Tucci speaks of joining Rally Software's executive team as, "It felt like coming home when I joined the company. There was a passion for people ahead of products and profits. The emphasis was on people, people, people, people, then products, then profits. We looked closely at what do people want at work. We found they want to be appreciated, get feedback, feel part of a team, and have a higher purpose with their work."

The negative feminine can be as bad, where a group is stuck in conversation, never moving forward to make a decision. An organization that is overly consensus driven is an example of the negative feminine.

Bottom line, too much of anything can be a bad thing. You need both. Can you imagine a roper with no horse? Tension comes into play when we, as leaders, approach everything as a problem to solve, as opposed to a polarity to manage.

Our job as gender-intelligent leaders is to manage the polarities across the individuals in the team to bring in the best of the masculine and feminine to the greatest outcome.

POLARITY OR PROBLEM?

The fundamental question I've learned to ask when encountering any business difficulty is: "Is this a problem we can solve, or is it an ongoing polarity we must manage well?"

Barry Johnson, author of the book, *Polarity Management: Identifying and Managing Unsolvable Problems*, wrote in a *Polarity Management Associates* article in 2012:

Polarities are energy pairs we can leverage in order to achieve success. We live in them and they live in us. We live in organizational polarities. They often show up as tough decisions or tensions: Should we centralize for system integration or decentralize to support entrepreneurial initiative? Should we preserve our core traditions or go after innovation? Also, leadership polarities live within us: Should we be clear or flexible? Should we be grounded or visionary?

With polarities, the answer is that we need both. To be effective with polarities, we need to use "AND" in our thinking. We need to leverage the benefits of centralization AND decentralization. When we use "OR" thinking to "solve" a polarity, we get in trouble. We are less likely to achieve the results we want.

Sounds like leveraging the strengths of the female and males in our business climate doesn't it?

I'M A GENDER-POLARITY-MANAGEMENT ROCK STAR!

Great leaders are good at their own polarity management. It isn't about compromising. It's about getting good at moving back and forth between the feminine and the masculine within ourselves when the situation requires it since each serves us in its own way.

Angela is a fabulous example of bringing the feminine to her business leadership. She describes her leadership philosophy this way: "My passion lies in what I can do to help people to have their best life, like John Wooden, the famous college basketball coach whose mission it was to make the best people, not just the best players. It's our responsibility as leaders to treat the whole employee, to build a thriving environment, thriving culture, eliminate fear and make it safe for people to be their best."

Jennifer Joyce worked for Amoco early in her career. She was new to continuous quality improvement. "Anything I brought up about quality improvement had the males in the room responding 'What's that got to do with the bottom line?' I wanted to scream, 'Screw the bottom line, quality is what's important.'"

Later as a wiser more knowledgeable professional, Jennifer realized the bottom line was as important as quality, and she was much better equipped to respond emphasizing the advantage of the *and* instead of *or*.

GENDER POLARITY SUMMARY POINTS

- If you only have access to one side of a polarity, you will absolutely fall into the negative of that polarity.
- Both sides of a polarity offer important and good stuff, but one without the other gets dysfunctional.
- It's *and*, not *or*.
- It's situational, not a compromise. When do you need feminine, when do you need masculine?

Managing gender polarity is a necessary business skill in the workplace, but it only provides women a glance into working well with men. I wish I'd had a guide to the male's attitudes about business when starting out.

As one who has played the be-like-a-man card in a room of men on more than one occasion, I have often asked myself if this take-no-prisoners attitude resulted in the 96 percent male-dominated CEO suite? Could this masculine attitude be the key to the impenetrable executive suite for 50 percent of women? In the 80s and 90s, some women tried being like the guys to fit in and succeed, but they were not successful in breaking the glass ceiling.

I know in my soul that our increased success does not lie in acting more like a man at work. The lack of authenticity always leaks out. When women try to act like men, business is missing out on the female influence that is necessary for getting business to a different outcome.

Taking the time to understand how each gender confronts work conflicts and problems differently gets us to the elusive pay dirt complement of working together.

Alain Paolini is a business consulting executive and a visible advocate for gender equality as co-chair of the Leadership Investment women's organization in Denver, Colorado. Alain shares an insider view of men in business when he confides, "Most men see corporate America as a game; the mission is to be as successful as possible. Whereas, women look at how they can maximize their contribution. Women promote others' needs over their own. They stay in the background when they feel there is a natural leader in the room. Men are trying to understand where they stand in the pecking order so they can take the place of the next guy."

Both genders have much to learn about understanding and better leveraging each other.

KEEP IT SIMPLE, STUPID

Alain's take on this difficult work seems simple. He says, "Help men help you. The majority of men are approachable, but they don't know how to help. Men don't think there is anything to fix. If you tell them what needs to be fixed, they will go fix it since they are good fixers. If you see a man who is hindering and not helping you, and you've clarified no malicious intent, ask for his help. Have the conversation."

On its website, a Connectria survey of US IT professionals found 83 percent of people have worked with a jerk within the last five years. So it's not if you're going to work with a jerk, it's when. But how do you handle the male colleague that might have malicious intent... or is just a jerk? Try matching the jerk's behavior.

When networking, *matching* or *mirroring* is the technique used to build rapport and make people comfortable more quickly. Research has shown that people who have rapport with each other display mirror image or matching body language.

You can also build rapport by matching body language. Visualize coming up to person at a networking event. As you start speaking to him or her, you cross your arms to mirror his arms being crossed. You lower the tone of your voice to match his quieter tone. If these mirroring actions are done discreetly, the person will not notice.

If you're lucky, he may comment how connected he feels talking to you, how he feels like you really get him, and that you're so easy to talk to. It's an unconscious reaction.

MIRROR, MIRROR ON THE WALL

I used this technique with a difficult male colleague who was a colorful yeller. He used swearing and being pushy to get his way. I tried everything in my female arsenal to find the path to less conflict and improve how we were working together—lowering my voice to remain the calm to his storm, treating him as the expert to elicit his help, being direct about how his communication style was impacting our getting to any common ground. Nothing worked.

One day at the end of my rope, I decided to mirror his behavior and strategically cursed right back at him. His eyes opened wide as he lowered his voice, and he paused then asked me what I thought we should do next. He was a bully and was waiting for me to stand up to him. I never had to raise my voice or curse again. Mirroring his behavior either unconsciously or consciously got him to recognize me as a peer on an even playing field.

Most professional women have acquired the skill of seeing the jerks coming; it's the subtler behaviors that challenge us.

DO STRONG WOMEN INTIMIDATE MEN?

According to Christopher Flett, author of *What Men Don't Tell Women about Business*, men are not intimidated by strong women. Flett says, "In fact, authentically powerful women impress men. Women who give up their power are not the real deal. You can't count on them consistently being strong. Men don't see alpha females as true equals because they assume they will sabotage themselves. Men respect women who don't give up their power to a man" (Flett 2008, 37).

Flett continues, "When a woman is authentically strong and holds herself in high esteem, the gender issue starts to dissolve, and she is considered an equal partner at the table" (Flett 2008, 38).

Debbie Brown, a high-powered consultant in the energy space, shared her advice, "I advise young women especially not to offer coffee to meeting attendees, no matter the gender. If you appear to be the secretary, you'll be treated like the secretary. Instead, act like the boss."

DO MEN SUFFER FROM IMPOSTOR SYNDROME?

Impostor Syndrome is a term coined in 1978 by clinical psychologists, Dr. Pauline R. Clance and Suzanne A. Imes. They wrote, "Despite outstanding academic and professional accomplishments, women who experience the imposter phenomenon persist in believing that they are really not bright and have fooled anyone who thinks otherwise."

Clance and Imes were the first to suggest that the impostor syndrome is particularly common among high-achieving women in their 1978 study (Clance and Imes 1978. 241-247), while a 2013 study by Lucas Laursen indicates that men and women are equally affected (Laursen 2013).

Michael Frendo, head of engineering at Polycom, contributes his perspective, "Most men don't suffer to the same level with the impostor syndrome. Some men believe they can do anything and can figure it out as they go, yet they can be the most unaware and incompetent men you'll ever meet. They've been trained all along that there is nothing they aren't good at or can't be good at."

Christopher Flett adds, "Everyday CEOs throughout the world get up and ask themselves the question, *Is today the day they find out I don't know what I'm doing?"* (Flett 2008, 59). It's one of the reasons men can become aggressive when they receive criticism or feedback. Knowing this about men can help women approach them in a direct but compassionate way. It shouldn't keep us from speaking our mind but rather provide feedback in a way that emphasizes the link to the success of the business.

Alain Paolini offers, "The vast majority of men aren't aware of how their behavior is negatively impacting women. Great feedback might go like this, 'Alain, when we're in a meeting and you say XYX, it makes me feel ABC, and as a result, I disengage and I feel others around you might disengage.' If I'm Alain, I'm going to be thankful." With our help, men will develop better radar for what they can do to help women be successful.

DO WOMEN AND MEN SUPPORT EACH OTHER DIFFERENTLY?

Silvia Travesani suggests, "Men have a better network. Men help each other so much, to the extent that even incompetent men can succeed. They ambitiously sell each other. Most of the men in high positions aren't that special—they are average. Women work harder. We study more. Because of that, I think we're ahead."

Silvia's attitude supports my own experience in the business arena; men support men because they are men and women support women in spite of them being women. We each have the responsibility to change this perception! A cowgirl is only as successful as her posse.

THE B WORD

Tina Fey said, "You're nobody until somebody calls you *bossy.*"

Men (and some women) call women bossy. I'd daresay a man has never had to deal with the self-doubt that comes from being called bossy. The word I've heard most in my career is *pushy.*

"Wendy is too pushy and aggressive." I heard this feedback from my boss after working with an especially difficult customer who was pushing *us* for free consulting.

I stood up to my boss with, "Our business benefits from the fact that I get told every once in a while that I'm pushy. It means I'm pushing the envelope in terms of us not being taken advantage of by the customer, in getting a fair price for what we're worth, and in valuing us as a business. I'm closing more deals because I'm going after it. That means there may be customers that see that as pushy."

I emphasized that if this feedback became more frequent, we might need to take a deeper look at my style. It still burned my britches that I even had to have this conversation since I strongly doubt a man would have had it.

In his many years of supporting women and men in high tech over the years, Michael Frendo sees women being as likely to say she's bossy and he's a leader. We each have our own brand of unconscious bias toward how women and men should act.

There was a controversial social campaign to make bossy a good thing for girls. Beyoncé had a YouTube video, *Ban Bossy—I'm Not*

Bossy. I'm the Boss. The video was all about flipping something negative to make it inspirational.

What if we could retrain our brains to see bossy as a positive attribute that would serve our girls to make them better leaders? That's exactly what I was trying to do with my boss's conversation about my being pushy.

I NEED ONE MORE CLASS, AND I'LL BE READY

A Hewlett Packard internal report stated that men apply for a job when they meet only 60 percent of the qualifications, but women apply only if they meet 100 percent of them (Mohr 2014). Women wait to be overqualified for a role, presentation, or assignment before they go for a job or promotion.

Men approach the same situation with an attitude of *you don't need to know everything; you just need to know more than your clients. And if you don't know, it's your job to find out faster than they can find out you don't know what you are talking about.*

As we saw earlier, the tendency to look too harshly on our capabilities or actions is a common trait of women having highly active cingulate gyri. This is the neurological reason women self-rate lower than men. It can also lead women to beat themselves up for no reason. This awareness can liberate women and remind gender-intelligent men to downplay inaccurate self-assessments of their female employees. When women realize that others are going for a job even when every qualification is not met, they feel empowered to do the same.

In her no nonsense way, Jean Becker, CTO at Accenture, talks about the importance of confidence in your own abilities. She coins it *swagger*, and she's not talking about that egotistical conceited swagger of the rodeo cowboy who thinks he's God's gift to the audience. It's the ability to sit down with a client, have the conversation, and not have to be prepared with all the answers before going in. Have the confidence that you can figure out whatever is in that moment, and know you're sufficient to get it done. Navigate the situation with swagger and, if called for, a little sassy hand on your hip for flavor.

WRAP IT UP, JOHNNY

A gender-balanced workplace evolves when men take advantage of the powerful qualities of women, and women strategically leverage the strength of men.

The negative masculine status quo of business is no longer serving us. There is no simple fix. A gender-intelligent workplace is going to require a different solution. Consider the rancher who finds the price of cattle falling consistently over several years. She must rethink her revenue model. She adds bison and free-range chickens to her livestock holdings, capturing the healthy eating trend. Business is at this exact same place.

It takes creativity, hard work, and sweat to create a gender-balanced culture that leverages both male and female players to be better by working together in a more complementary manner.

If you don't get anything else, businesses leader, get this. You must acquire three or more women for your board to gain the financial impact of gender intelligence. You must assess representation and retention of women in your business, commit to equal pay, and create measurable gender-equality initiatives. And you must attack gender bias in your organization with the same tenacity used to innovate product development.

Every cowgirl and cowboy must step up to change our current normal. We must readjust as we approach every decision to create a climate where men and women have the exact same potential for success in the workplace. Gender equality is not *a nice to have*. It is a *must have*! Cowboy and Cowgirl Up to this challenge with the tenacity of someone who won't quit. It's a long, rocky, steep trail, but the view is worth it.

THE COWGIRL'S
CORPORATE TRAIL RIDE CHECKLIST

o   A Pair of Field Glasses—Perspective to remember the positive of your past and highlight the promise of the trail ahead

o   A Piece of Leather—Cowgirl gumption to bite down on when doing the right thing is harder than doing the easy thing

o   A Bullwhip—Quick wit and style to put the disgusting renegades in their place when the need arises

o   Your Favorite Cowgirl Hat—Passion for being clear with your unique brand and making a difference in the world

o   A Comfortable Pair of Cowgirl Boots—Versatility to roll through the changes in your career with class and style

o   A Broken-In Saddle—A cowgirl posse you can count on, including at least one mentor inside and outside your company

o   A Respected Trail Boss—At least one sponsor to put you forward for the bigger jobs

o   A Plug of Chew—Energy to create an exceptional culture so those following you feel successful because of who they are, not in spite of it

o   Your Faithful Mustang—At least one trusted cowboy in your corner to tell you the tough stuff

REFERENCES

Beckel, Bob, Thomas, Cal. 2007. "Gender Games." Inside News, *USA Today*. November 28.
http://usatoday30.usatoday.com/printedition/news/20071128/co mmonlede.art.htm.

Brown, Brené. 2010. "Brené Brown: The Power of Vulnerability." TedXHouston. June.
https://www.ted.com/talks/brene_brown_on_vulnerability?lang uage=en#t-94406.

Boyd, Todd. 2007. "The O Factor." *Richmond Times Dispatch*. December 2.

Brewer, Marilynn B. 1979. "In-Group Bias in the Minimal Intergroup Situation: A Cognitive-Motivational Analysis." *Psychological Bulletin* 86: 307–324. http://dx.doi.org/10.1037/0033-2909.86.2.307.

Casnocha, Ben. 2007. *My Start-Up Life*. San Francisco: John Wiley & Sons, Inc.

Clance, Pauline Rose, and Imes, Suzanne A. 1978. "The Imposter Phenomenon in High Achieving Women: Dynamics and Therapeutic Intervention." *Psychotherapy: Theory, Research and Practice* 15 (3): 241–247.
http://www.paulineroseclance.com/pdf/ip_high_achieving_wo men.pdf.

Dahl, Melissa. 2015. "Why Do Women Cry More Than Men?" *Science of Us.* January 7. http://nymag.com/scienceofus/2015/01/why-do-women-cry-more-than-men.html.

Delaney, Laurel. 2007. "Are We Our Own Worst Enemy?" *Divapreneurs.* July/August.

Deutschendorf, Harvey. 2016. "7 Reasons Why Emotional Intelligence Is One of the Fastest-Growing Job Skills." *Fast Company.* May 4. http://www.fastcompany.com/3059481/7-reasons-why-emotional-intelligence-is-one-of-the-fastest-growing-job-skills.

Female Factor, The. 2015. "Stats & Facts: Women by the Numbers." Accessed November 1. http://www.thefemalefactor.com/statistics/statistics_about_women.html.

Flett, Christopher. 2008. *What Men Don't Tell Women about Business*. Hoboken: John Wiley & Sons, Inc.

Frisk, Adam. 2015. "'Because It's 2015': Trudeau's Gender-Equal Cabinet Makes Headlines Around World, Social Media." *Global News.* November 5. http://globalnews.ca/news/2320795/because-its-2015-trudeaus-gender-equal-cabinet-makes-headlines-around-world-social-media.

Gurian, Michael, and Barbara Annis. 2008. *Leadership and the Sexes*. San Francisco: Jossey-Bass.

Johnson, Barry. 2012. "Leveraging Polarities Summary." April 6.
http://www.margaretseidler.com/wp-content/uploads/2014/01/ArticleLeveragingPolaritiesSummary
BarryJohnson2012.pdf.

Lanpher, Katherine. 2007. "Climb the Ladder or Build Your Own."
More Magazine, September.

Laursen, Lucas. 2013. "No, You're Not an Imposter." *Science Careers*. Oct. http://www.sciencemag.org/careers/2008/02/no-youre-not-impostor.

Mohr, Tara Sophia. 2014. "Why Women Don't Apply for Jobs Unless They're 100% Qualified." *Harvard Business Review*. August 25. https://hbr.org/2014/08/why-women-dont-apply-for-jobs-unless-theyre-100-qualified.

Noonan, Peggy. 2007. "Things are Tough All Over." Opinion section, *Wall Street Journal*. November 10. http://www.wsj.com/articles/SB119464195121588274.

Rigoglioso, Marguerite. 2006. "Diverse Backgrounds and Personalities Can Strengthen Groups." *Insights by Stanford Business*. August 1. https://www.gsb.stanford.edu/insights/diverse-backgrounds-personalities-can-strengthen-groups.

Rosato, Donna. 2015. "Surprising Secrets of Successful Second-Act Career Changers." *Money*. April 16. http://time.com/money/3824074/second-act-careers.

Ryan, K. M., King, E. B., Adis, C., Gulick, L. M. V., Peddie, C., and Hargraves, R. 2012. "Exploring the Asymmetrical Effects of Gender Tokenism on Supervisor-Subordinate Relationships."

November 16. *Journal of Applied Social Psychology* 42: 56–102. doi:10.1111/j.1559-1816.2012.01025.x.

Schillaci, Sophie. 2015. "Bradley Cooper Stands by Jennifer Lawrence Over Equal Pay in Hollywood: 'There Is a Double Standard.'" *ET Online.* October 13. http://www.etonline.com/news/173916_bradley_cooper_stands _by_jennifer_lawrence_over_equal_pay_hollywood_there_is_a _double_standard.

Smith Brain Trust. 2015. "A Hidden Quota for Women in Top Management." *News at Smith.* March 25. http://www.rhsmith.umd.edu/news/hidden-quota-women-top-management.

Watson, Emma. 2014. "Gender Equality Is Your Issue Too." *UN Women.* September 20. http://www.unwomen.org/en/news/stories/2014/9/emma-watson-gender-equality-is-your-issue-too.

INTERVIEWEE LIST

1. Mary Baum, president, BA&T
2. Jean Becker, managing director, Accenture
3. Debbie Brown, consultant, Coloradans for Responsible Energy Development
4. Cheryl Campbell, SVP, Xcel Energy
5. Michael Frendo, SVP engineering, Polycom
6. Bill Hoberecht, owner, Pinnacle Performance
7. Kathy Hodgson, city manager, City of Lakewood
8. Jennifer Joyce, cofounder/partner, Leadership Smarts
9. Tiffany Kelly, CEO, Ed10x
10. Margaret McLean, general counsel and chief risk officer, TeleTech
11. Alain Paolini, vice president, enVision Business Consulting
12. Kristin Russell, president, Arrow Electronics
13. Praful Shah, angel investor
14. Robin Szeliga, management consultant
15. Silvia Travesani, cofounder, BeVisible Powered by Latina Millennials
16. Angela Tucci, executive, CA Technologies
17. Annette Quintana, owner, Istonish Holding Company
18. Roxanne Varza, director, Halle Freyssinet

Bring *Cowgirl Up!* to Your

Organization

KEYNOTES

Wendy Bohling is an engaging and inspirational speaker able to connect with a group of five to fifteen hundred. She pushes audiences to rethink their status quo, inspiring them to push their boundaries. As an extroverted engineer, she is especially effective with mixed-gender and female audiences who work in male-dominated industries.

In addition to keynote presentations showcasing the concepts from *Corporate Cowgirl Up! A Woman's Guide to Navigating the Corporate Frontier,* Wendy and her team deliver a wide range of gender intelligence and leadership topics. The following are just a few of the sessions:

- Mind the Gap: The Journey to a Gender Intelligent Workplace
- The Unbiased Gender Lens: Busting Bias in Your Organization
- Locking Down Your Female A-Players
- Gender Lens Networking
- Gender Intelligent Negotiating—How Men and Women Negotiate Differently
- Power Networking for Introverts
- Engineering Passion in Your Career and Life
- Engineering Life Balance
- Gender Intelligent Communication Skills (for women) (for men)
- You've Got the Power (for women)
- Be the Trail Boss of Your Career

Your attendees will leave your event with actionable steps and the tools to move the dial in your organization immediately.

We are always adding topics. We would love to work with you to customize a topic to fit your specific needs.

www.corporatecowgirlup.com/speaking

WORKSHOPS

Cowgirl Up! is available as a powerful workshop experience. Seasoned Corporate Cowgirl Up facilitators will partner with you throughout the planning process to ensure that the workshop supports your strategic priorities.

The ability in your business to leverage, build, and retain exceptional leaders is the single biggest key to meeting your strategic objectives. Baseline your current leadership development process with our Mind the Gap™ leadership assessment.

Our team will work with you to develop a customized leadership training plan to attack those areas holding you back. Gain insightful gender intelligence leadership training to take your team to the next level of financial and innovation results.

Participant Benefits:
- Articulate why gender-intelligent culture matters—business and professional development impact.
- Apply the Mind the Gap™ assessment to diagnose the health of your organization or your talent development program.
- Detailed strategic plan to develop and manage your organization initiatives.

Target Audience:
- Association Conferences and Meetings
- Cross Corporate Teamwork Programs
- Executive Leadership Development Programs
- High Performance Female Talent Retention Programs
- Corporate Women's Conferences (tech and male-dominated industries a special focus)
- Leadership Retreats and Summits
- Leaders and Employees Professional Coaching

www.corporatecowgirlup.com/speaking

ORGANIZATIONAL AND
GENDER INTELLIGENCE CONSULTING

An inclusive, diverse culture is shown to achieve better business results, more engaged employees, and higher innovation. Gender diversity is especially difficult to achieve in male-dominated industries such as technology, energy, oil/gas, and automotive. CEOs in these industries are purposely setting new goals around gender parity. Not only because it's the right thing to do but, more importantly, so they can capture the financial benefits to the business.

An inclusive culture requires competence to understand the conscious and unconscious bias in an organization. Our *Mind the Gap*™ Gender Equality Audit will baseline the five key areas seen as crucial to competence for an inclusive culture and highlight via a heat map the areas most impactful for change.

- Quantitative data by gender, race, sexual orientation and age for the following key metric areas:
    - Business-wide demographics of the business, both in total and at each level.
    - Retention of staff
    - Succession planning
    - Raises and promotion rates of your staff
- Review of performance feedback process
- Hiring practices
- Interviews with a cross segment of population
- Exit interviews

Contact us today to explore how a partnership with Corporate Cowgirl Up could transform your results. E-mail us at info@corporatecowgirlup.com or call us at +1-303-500-6861.

www.corporatecowgirlup.com/programs

ABOUT THE AUTHOR

Wendy Hall Bohling is a sought-after speaker, thought leader, and corporate consultant on gender intelligence and inclusive leadership. Her academic credentials include a BS in mathematics and an MS in computer science.

She is CEO of Corporate Cowgirl Up. Wendy has more than thirty years as an executive in the corporate saddle at some of the top telecom Fortune 100 companies and healthcare IT start-ups.

The journey from computer engineer to social scientist and the vast diversity in her professional life revealed her passion for this bigger work of building gender-intelligent leaders to drive increased profitability and innovation in business.

Growing up in a small town in Virginia gave Wendy an appreciation for neighbors who watch out for each other and for family that always has your back. She lives out her cowgirl dream in the beautiful mountains of Colorado. She shares her life with her son and daughter and her favorite enlightened cowboy, Chris.

If this book helped you in some way, please consider leaving a review. Reach out to me to share what additional insight or information might be helpful in your career journey.

@corpcowgirlup corpcowgirlup

wendy@corporatecowgirlup.com